W9-AAE-135

Bloom's BioCritiques

Bloom's BioCritiques

CHARLES DICKENS

Edited and with an introduction by
Harold Bloom
Sterling Professor of the Humanities
Yale University

CHELSEA HOUSE
PUBLISHERS
A Haights Cross Communications Company
Philadelphia

©2003 by Chelsea House Publishers, a subsidiary of
Haights Cross Communications.

A Haights Cross Communications Company

Introduction © 2003 by Harold Bloom.

Printed and bound in the United States of America

10 9 8 7 6 5 4 3 2 1

Library of Congress Cataloging-in-Publication Data

Charles Dickens / Harold Bloom, editor ; Mei Chin, contributing editor.
    p. cm. — (Bloom's biocritiques)
"Works by Charles Dickens": p.
Includes bibliographical references (p.) and index.
  ISBN 0-7910-6365-8
  1. Dickens, Charles, 1812-1870—Criticism and interpretation. I.
Bloom, Harold. II. Chin, Mei. III. Series.
  PR4588 .C358 2002
  823'.8—dc21

                        2002007683

Chelsea House Publishers
1974 Sproul Road, Suite 400
Broomall, PA 19008-0914

http://www.chelseahouse.com

Contributing editor: Mei Chin

Cover credit: Hulton Getty/Liaison Agency

Cover Design by Keith Trego

Layout by EJB Publishing Services

CONTENTS

User's Guide

These volumes are designed to introduce the reader to the life and work of the world's literary masters. Each volume begins with Harold Bloom's essay "The Work in the Writer" and a volume-specific introduction also written by Professor Bloom. Following these unique introductions is an engaging biography that discusses the major life events and important literary accomplishments of the author under consideration.

Furthermore, each volume includes an original critique that not only traces the themes, symbols, and ideas apparent in the author's works, but strives to put those works into a cultural and historical perspective. In addition to the original critique is a brief selection of significant critical essays previously published on the author and his or her works followed by a concise and informative chronology of the writer's life. Finally, each volume concludes with a bibliography of the writer's works, a list of additional readings, and an index of important themes and ideas.

HAROLD BLOOM

The Work in the Writer

Literary biography found its masterpiece in James Boswell's *Life of Samuel Johnson.* Boswell, when he treated Johnson's writings, implicitly commented upon Johnson as found in his work, even as in the great critic's life. Modern instances of literary biography, such as Richard Ellmann's lives of W. B. Yeats, James Joyce, and Oscar Wilde, essentially follow in Boswell's pattern.

That the writer somehow is in the work, we need not doubt, though with William Shakespeare, writer-of-writers, we almost always need to rely upon pure surmise. The exquisite rancidities of the Problem Plays or Dark Comedies seem to express an extraordinary estrangement of Shakespeare from himself. When we read or attend *Troilus and Cressida* and *Measure for Measure,* we may be startled by particular speeches of Ulysses in the first play, or of Vincentio in the second. These speeches, of Ulysses upon hierarchy or upon time, or of Duke Vincentio upon death, are too strong either for their contexts or for the characters of their speakers. The same phenomenon occurs with Parolles, the military impostor of *All's Well That Ends Well.* Utterly disgraced, he nevertheless affirms: "Simply the thing I am/Shall make me live."

In Shakespeare, more even than in his peers, Dante and Cervantes, meaning always starts itself again through excess or overflow. The strongest of Shakespeare's creatures—Falstaff, Hamlet, Iago, Lear, Cleopatra—have an exuberance that is fiercer than their plays can contain. If Ben Jonson was at all correct in his complaint that "Shakespeare wanted art," it could have been only in a sense that he may not have intended. Where do the personalities of Falstaff or Hamlet touch a limit? What was it in Shakespeare that made the two parts of *Henry IV* and *Hamlet* into "plays unlimited"? Neither Falstaff nor Hamlet will be stopped: their wit, their beautiful, laughing speech, their intensity of being—all these are virtually infinite.

In what ways do Falstaff and Hamlet manifest the writer in the work? Evidently, we can never know, or know enough to answer with any authority. But what would happen if we reversed the question, and asked: How did the work form the writer, Shakespeare?

Of Shakespeare's inwardness, his biography tells us nothing. And yet, to an astonishing extent, Shakespeare created our inwardness. At the least, we can speculate that Shakespeare so lived his life as to conceal the depths of his nature, particularly as he rather prematurely aged. We do not have Shakespeare on Shakespeare, as any good reader of the Sonnets comes to realize: they do not constitute a key that unlocks his heart. No sequence of sonnets could be less confessional or more powerfully detached from the poet's self.

The German poet and universal genius, Goethe, affords a superb contrast to Shakespeare. Of Goethe's life, we know more than everything; I wonder sometimes if we know as much about Napoleon or Freud or any other human being who ever has lived, as we know about Goethe. Everywhere, we can find Goethe in his work, so much so that Goethe seems to crowd the writing out, just as Byron and Oscar Wilde seem to usurp their own literary accomplishments. Goethe, cunning beyond measure, nevertheless invested a rival exuberance in his greatest works that could match his personal charisma. The sublime outrageousness of the Second Part of *Faust*, or of the greater lyric and meditative poems, form a Counter-Sublime to Goethe's own daemonic intensity.

Goethe was fascinated by the daemonic in himself; we can doubt that Shakespeare had any such interests. Evidently, Shakespeare abandoned his acting career just before he composed *Measure for Measure* and *Othello*. I surmise that the egregious interventions by Vincentio and Iago displace the actor's energies into a new kind of mischief-making, a fresh opening to a subtler playwriting-within-the-play.

But what had opened Shakespeare to this new awareness? The answer is the work in the writer, *Hamlet* in Shakespeare. One can go further: it was not so much the play, *Hamlet*, as the character Hamlet, who changed Shakespeare's art forever.

Hamlet's personality is so large and varied that it rivals Goethe's own. Ironically Goethe's Faust, his Hamlet, has no personality at all, and is as colorless as Shakespeare himself seems to have chosen to be. Yet nothing could be more colorful than the Second Part of *Faust*, which is peopled by an astonishing array of monsters, grotesque devils, and classical ghosts.

A contrast between Shakespeare and Goethe demonstrates that in each—but in very different ways—we can better find the work in the person, than we can discover that banal entity, the person in the work. Goethe to many of his contemporaries, seemed to be a mortal god. Shakespeare, so far as we know, seemed an affable, rather ordinary fellow, who aged early and became somewhat withdrawn. Yet Faust, though Mephistopheles battles for his soul, is hardly worth the trouble unless you take him as an idea and not as a person. Hamlet is nearly every-idea-in-one, but he is precisely a personality and a person.

Would Hamlet be so astonishingly persuasive if his father's ghost did not haunt him? Falstaff is more alive than Prince Hal, who says that the devil haunts him in the shape of an old fat man. Three years before composing the final *Hamlet*, Shakespeare invented Falstaff, who then never ceased to haunt his creator. Falstaff and Hamlet may be said to best represent the work in the writer, because their influence upon Shakespeare was prodigious. W. H. Auden accurately observed that Falstaff possesses infinite energy: never tired, never bored, and absolutely both witty and happy until Hal's rejection destroys him. Hamlet too has infinite energy, but in him it is more curse than blessing.

Falstaff and Hamlet can be said to occupy the roles in Shakespeare's invented world that Sancho Panza and Don Quixote possess in Cervantes's. Shakespeare's plays from 1610 on (starting with *Twelfth Night*) are thus analogous to the Second Part of Cervantes's epic novel. Sancho and the Don overtly jostle Cervantes for authorship in the Second Part, even as Cervantes battles against the impostor who has pirated a continuation of his work. As a dramatist, Shakespeare manifests the work in the writer more indirectly. Falstaff's prose genius is revived in the scapegoating of Malvolio by Maria and Sir Toby Belch, while Falstaff's darker insights are developed by Feste's melancholic wit. Hamlet's intellectual resourcefulness, already deadly, becomes poisonous in Iago and in Edmund. Yet we have not crossed into the deeper abysses of the work in the writer in later Shakespeare.

No fictive character, before or since, is Falstaff's equal in self-trust. Sir John, whose delight in himself is contagious, has total confidence both in his self-awareness and in the resources of his language. Hamlet, whose self is as strong, and whose language is as copious, nevertheless distrusts both the self and language. Later Shakespeare is, as it were, much under the influence both of Falstaff and of Hamlet, but they tug him in opposite directions. Shakespeare's own copiousness of language is well-nigh incredible: a vocabulary in excess of twenty-one thousand words, almost eighteen hundred of which he coined himself. And of his word-hoard, nearly half are used only once each, as though the perfect setting for each had been found, and need not be repeated. Love for language and faith in language are Falstaffian attributes. Hamlet will darken both that love and that faith in Shakespeare, and perhaps the Sonnets can best be read as Falstaff and Hamlet counterpointing against one another.

Can we surmise how aware Shakespeare was of Falstaff and Hamlet, once they had played themselves into existence? *Henry IV, Part I* appeared in six quarto editions during Shakespeare's lifetime; *Hamlet* possibly had four. Falstaff and Hamlet were played again and again at the Globe, but Shakespeare knew also that they were being read, and he must have had contact with some of those readers. What would it have been like to discuss Falstaff or Hamlet with one of their early readers (presumably also part of their audience at the Globe), if you were the creator of such demiurges? The question would seem nonsensical to most Shakespeare scholars, but then these days they tend to be either ideologues or moldy figs. How can we recover the uncanniness of Falstaff and of Hamlet, when they now have become so familiar?

A writer's influence upon himself is an unexplored problem in criticism, but such an influence is never free from anxieties. The biocritical problem (which this series attempts to explore) can be divided into two areas, difficult to disengage fully. Accomplished works affect the author's life, and also affect her subsequent writings. It is simpler for me to surmise the effect of *Mrs. Dalloway* and *To the Lighthouse* upon Woolf's late *Between the Acts*, than it is to relate Clarissa Dalloway's suicide and Lily Briscoe's capable endurance in art to the tragic death and complex life of Virginia Woolf.

There are writers whose lives were so vivid that they seem sometimes to obscure the literary achievement: Byron, Wilde, Malraux, Hemingway. But most major Western writers do not live that exuberantly, and the greatest of all, Shakespeare, sometimes appears to have adopted the personal mask of colorlessness. And yet there are heroes of literature who struggled titanically with their own eras—Tolstoy, Milton, Victor Hugo—who nevertheless matter more for their works than their lives.

There are great figures—Emily Dickinson, Wallace Stevens, Willa Cather—who seem to have had so little of the full intensity of life when compared to the vitality of their work, that we might almost speak of the work in the work, rather than even of the work in a person. Emily Brontë might well be the extreme instance of such a visionary, surpassing William Blake in that one regard.

I conclude this general introduction to a series of literary bio-critiques by stating a tentative formula or principle for gauging the many ways in which the work influences the person and her subsequent, later work. Our influence upon ourselves is always related to the Shakespearean invention of self-overhearing, which I have written about in several other contexts. Life, as well as poetry and prose, is overheard rather than simply heard. The writer listens to herself as though she were somebody else, and the will to change begins to operate. The forces that live in us include the prior work we have done, and the dreams and waking visions that evade our dismissals.

HAROLD BLOOM

Introduction

Charles Dickens began with *The Pickwick Papers* and ended his progression of novels with the unfinished *Mystery of Edwin Drood*, published posthumously in 1870, after the novelist's death at fifty-eight. His best novels certainly include *Oliver Twist, Nicholas Nickleby, Martin Chuzzlewitt, Dombey and Son, David Copperfield,* and *Bleak House,* generally judged his masterpiece. *Hard Times,* though critically esteemed, has not enjoyed a wide public, unlike *A Tale of Two Cities,* an immense success with ordinary readers rather than with critics. *Great Expectations* pleases all however, while *Our Mutual Friend,* despite its comic splendor, has been less famous. I have omitted *Little Dorrit,* which would be another novelist's masterwork.

It is impossible not to find Dickens' life in his work, but I will maintain my emphasis here on the work in the writer. So large is Dickens, who created a world, that one has to be very selective in brooding upon him. He possessed, in the highest degree, what John Ruskin credited in him: "stage fire." Though not a dramatist (his play *The Frozen Deep,* with Wilkie Collins, is still-born) Dickens was a remarkable public performer. His commercial readings from his own fiction, with the novelist acting all the roles, were highly successful but dangerously exhausting, and helped to kill him at fifty-eight.

One should not underestimate Dickens' theatrical gifts and interests. He thought nothing of directing, acting in, and touring with a play by Ben Jonson while continuing his intense novelistic career. Yet his extraordinary readings from his own work, which overwhelmed audiences, drained him, and cost us the books he might have written, after he turned fifty-eight.

Dickens was at his most passionate and personal in *David Copperfield* and *Great Expectations*, where David and Pip are all but self-portraits of the young Dickens. The effect of Dickens-the-novelist on portraits of the novelist as a young man is profound, but the autobiographical element is so strong as to indicate primarily the traditional mode of the life transmuted into literature. My quarry is subtler: the influence of Dickens' creative mind upon itself. I turn therefore to what is unsurpassable in him: *Bleak House*.

As a representation of Dickens' visionary cosmos, *Bleak House* is a vast romance-structure, free of any overt Dickens-surrogates. Esther Summerson is wonderfully sympathetic, and in a complex way she is a portrait of Dickens' Muse, his sister-in-law, Georgina Hogarth, who pragmatically presided over the Dickens household. If Dickens' imagination is directly represented in *Bleak House*, it can only be by Esther Summerson.

Esther stands apart from the other central characters, who emerge from what critics have learned to call: "The Dickens world." Great grotesques throng the chapters: the benignly idealized paternal figure, John Jarndyce; the wicked, madly attractive, and murderous Hortense, the sublime bloodhound, Inspector Bucket; the Leigh Hunt parody of Skimpole; the parody of Savage Landor in Boythorn. If one adds the fantastics–Mrs. Jellyby, Miss Flute, Mr. Krook (who goes up in spontaneous combustion), and best of all Lady Dedlock, you find yourself surrounded by creatures of an invented world that both entertains and disturbs. The Dickens cosmos precedes *Bleak House*, yet its entrance into this book is marked by a difference. Composing *Bleak House*, Dickens experiences the dramatic urgency of his earlier adventures into the self and into otherness.

MARIE TENNENT SHEPHARD

Biography of Charles Dickens

A Christmas Carol

When Charles Dickens took up his pen in mid-October of 1843 to write the first of his yearly Christmas stories, the spirit of the coming season was already upon him. *A Christmas Carol* overflows with images of winter snow, plum pudding, roasted goose, sounds of chestnuts crackling in the fire, and red holly berries—all emblems of a time of year the author loved—and the work itself now has become emblematic of the very season. Dickens, whose strain of gothicism was never quite out of view, called *Carol* "this Ghostly little book."

In his *Sketches by Boz*, Dickens wrote, "There seems to be a magic in the very name of Christmas." From a chapter in *The Pickwick Papers* about a Christmas at Dingley Dell comes a similar estimation: "Happy, happy Christmas, that can win us back to the delusions of our childish days, that can recall to the old man the pleasures of his youth!"

Apart from his enthusiasm for the season's joys, Dickens had other motives for writing the book. He was passionate about social reform and committed to showing to the reading public the desperate need for outreach to the less fortunate members of Victorian society. He had recently visited a "Ragged School"—an institution that provided a basic education to children of the poor—which he'd referred to as "an awful sight." (Johnson, 461) The school was a crude place, and Dickens had found its pupils ignorant, filthy, and badly dressed; he warned that the appalling conditions would drive these urchins to a life of crime. "I have very seldom seen," he said of the school, "in all the strange and dreadful things I have seen in London and elsewhere, anything so shocking as to the dire neglect of soul and body exhibited among these children." (461) He addressed the necessity for decent buildings and hygienic facilities: sinks must be installed, and soap and towels provided, so that the children would at least be clean to begin the day.

But Dickens had another reason for writing the story: he too needed money. The novel he had in the works, *Martin Chuzzlewit*, a serial of twenty monthly installments, was disappointing its publishers by sluggish sales, and Chapman and Hall mentioned the possible necessity of reducing their payments to him. When Dickens heard this, he "promptly went through at least two ceilings, the roof, and well into mid-air" (Johnson, 456); his books had made Chapman and Hall one of the most successful publishing companies in London, and he came to call them "bitter bad judges of an author" and "scaly-headed vultures." That this came at a time when he had outstanding bills made him angrier than ever; he said to his friend John Forster, "I am so irritated, so rubbed in the tenderest part of my eyelids with bay-salt, by what I told you yesterday that a wrong kind of fire is burning in my head, and I don't think I *can* write." (456)

Dickens had been born to financial woe. When his debt-ridden father borrowed money from Charles, he seldom found it necessary to pay his son back. The arrival of a fifth child in Charles Dickens' own household made further demands on an already depleted income. Dickens decided that a short book that he could put out quickly and sell at a moderate price would bring in enough to pay off his debts.

Dickens wrote his "Ghostly little book" for the money, then, and from some larger sense of social consciousness; but the effect of his work is on another order of magnitude entirely. Some have suggested that Dickens *invented* the modern idea of Christmas. He had written at length on the subject. When he created *A Christmas Carol*, with its theme of selfishness, greed, and benevolence, he must have hoped to share the magic he felt. To Scrooge's "bah humbug" and snarling conviction that "every idiot who goes about with 'Merry Christmas' on his lips should be boiled with his own pudding and buried with a stake of holly through his heart," Bob Cratchit replies, "I am sure I have always thought of Christmas time, when it has come round ... as a good time; a kind, forgiving, charitable, pleasant time; the only time I know of, in the long calendar of the year, when men and women seem by one consent to open their shut-up hearts freely ..." At the end of the book, when through his trials Scrooge has become generous, he tells his clerk, "A Merry Christmas, Bob! ... I'll raise your salary, and endeavor to assist your struggling family ..." This is Dickens' own vision of mankind's change for the better.

Dickens told his friend, advisor, and mentor, John Forster, that he had written the little book in a fever of excitement, "wept over it ... laughed, and wept again"; Forster himself noted that "no one was more fond than Dickens of old nursery tales." (Johnson, 410) Dickens had spent many nights in the foggy streets of London thinking about it. Sights he recalled when he had wandered there as a lonely, hungry boy appeared as Scrooge's childhood in Christmas Past.

The author had set himself a deadline to have the book completed within six weeks, for *Carol* had to be in the shops before Christmas and must be produced according to his precise instructions. He ordered that its gilt-edged pages be bound in red cloth, and that the volume include eight illustrations, four of which were to be colored by hand. He wanted to present to his readers a handsome volume at a modest price. He would pay for the printing himself, against his royalties.

An enthusiastic public purchased 6,000 copies of *A Christmas Carol* on the first day. "I broke out like a madman," Dickens told a friend. "Such dinings, such dancings, such conjurings, such blind-man's buffings, such theater-goings, such kissings-out of old years, and kissings-in of new ones, never took place in these parts before." (Johnson, 467) He threw himself deliriously into Christmas. One critic wrote to Dickens, "You have done more good by this little publication, fostered more kindly feelings. And prompted more positive acts of beneficence." (Forster, 345)

Dickens was ecstatic. Books continued to sell by the thousands, and letters of praise arrived daily. *A Christmas Carol* soared. His troubles behind him, surely he could pay off those mounting debts.

Unfortunately, he had set the price at five shillings, disastrously low for such an item. When the figures came in for the sales of *Carol*, the author was devastated. He had planned to pay his debts with an expected profit of at least £1,000, but the fifteen thousand copies sold by the year's end had grossed just under £700, and the expensive publication costs would take a large share of that. Dickens moaned that all he had left from his great success was despair and disappointment.

Scenes of debtor's prison, where his family had lived in his earlier years, loomed large in his imagination once again.

To add to his woes, a twopenny weekly, *Parley's Illuminated Library* committed a literary theft by plagiarizing *A Christmas Carol*. Dickens brought suit but was forced to pay £700 in court costs when the "vagabonds" declared bankruptcy. American plagiarists, impractical to sue, were also stealing *Carol*, to satisfy the English-speaking public's voracious appetite for Dickens; the well-intentioned book was proving very expensive indeed. (Soon after this, Dickens would begin a crusade for international copyright law.)

Worried, but not completely crushed, Dickens made plans. When he finished the next installment of *Chuzzlewit*, he would rent out the house, pack up his wife, five children, the servants, and dog Timber, and leave for a more economical life in Italy.

The first adaptations of *Carol* appeared on London stages a few weeks after its publication. Although Dickens cringed at some of the butchered dramatizations of his work, they did serve to further his fame throughout Britain. And the productions reached those unable to read or who could not afford the book. A seventeenth-century invention, the magic lantern, was used to project the text onto surfaces where larger audiences could read it and see at the illustrations. In later years, artwork of scenes (such as Bob Cratchit's Christmas dinner) was photographed, then put onto slides and projected onto a screen.

Dickens read *Carol* in public more that one hundred times, and the work quickly became a juggernaut. But perhaps Dickens summarized his intentions best in his preface to it:

> I Have endeavored in this Ghostly little book to raise the Ghost of an idea, which shall not put my readers out of humour with themselves, with each other, with the season, or with me. May it haunt their houses pleasantly, and no one wish to lay it.

DICKENS' YOUTH IN PORTSMOUTH

In a small house on Mile End Terrace in Portsea, Charles Dickens was born, on February 7, 1812. Newspapers did not usually print news of births at that time, but John Dickens proudly announced in the local paper that a son had been born to him and his wife, Elizabeth; Charles was junior to the fifteen-month-old Fanny and would be followed by eight more siblings. He was christened Charles John Huffam, after his godfather, Christopher Huffam; but he never used his middle names or forgave his parents for them. The modest Dickens home on the outskirts of Portsmouth, on the southern coast of England, was one of a row of attached houses with small squares of garden in the front and back.

John Dickens worked as a clerk in the Navy Pay Office at the Portsmouth dockyard. A well-liked fellow, generous and warm-hearted, he often had the other clerks laughing at his jokes and stories. He received regular pay raises that should have allowed him to provide well for his family, but he was never able to manage his finances.

By the time Dickens was ten years old, he was aware of his family's financial problems. At the age of eleven, he learned his way around pawnshops, and at twelve he discovered he had to either make sixteen shillings last a week—about the wage of a sailor, but stretched for a family—or go hungry. (The value of the pound at that point in the century is difficult both to determine and to compare to that of the modern dollar; according to historian Daniel Pool estimates have varied greatly setting Dickens' weekly income at about $16, $40, or $160.)

John's parents had been servants at Crewe Hall, the home of Lord Crewe, Member of Parliament. John had been raised in luxury, amid elegant furnishings, carriages, and liverymen—all the trappings of the well-to-do. Lord Crewe had seen to the education of John and his older brother William and had helped John to obtain the post at the Navy Pay Office.

John had left Crewe Hall at nineteen, expecting wealth to be readily available. But on his modest salary, the lifestyle he had known as a child exceeded his means. Still, he liked to dress in fashion and appear as of a higher social station, and he spent freely on fine clothes, good food, and wine. Always the gentlemanly host, he took great pleasure in mixing a bowl of hot punch for a houseful of guests. He spent extravagantly and borrowed frequently.

He had married the daughter of Charles Barrow, a man who held a high position in the Pay Office. John felt that in marrying he had climbed up a step from his background as the son of servants. Elizabeth Barrow was pretty, affectionate, and energetic, and she loved to dance. Unfortunately, she was as impractical with money as her husband.

Before Charles was six months old, John was compelled to move the family to a house on Hawk Street, in a poorer section of Portsea; in all, Dickens would live in some twenty locations in his first twenty years, and descriptions based on his memories of these places, and of the people who lived in them, would turn up in his work. Was the keeper of the lodging-house on Hawk Street a model for Mrs. Pipchin in *Dombey and Son*? Charles' sister Fanny, after reading the book exclaimed, "Good heavens! What does this mean? You have painted our lodging-house-keeper and you were but two years old at the time." (Ackroyd, 16) The lodging-house lady, always dressed in black, might have made an impression on the toddler. (In *Dombey*, Mrs. Pipchin's husband has been dead for forty years; nevertheless she "still wore black bombazeen, of such a lusterless, deep, dead, somber shade, that gas itself couldn't light her up after dark ...") Dickens believed that "it was a mistake to fancy children ever forgot anything."

"I was a child of close observation," Dickens later said. "I looked at nothing that I know of, but saw everything." (Ackroyd, 14–15)

By 1814, the Portsmouth Pay Office closed and John Dickens received orders to report to London. The move meant a decrease in pay, since he would no longer receive an Outport Allowance. Elizabeth's sister Mary joined them and contributed a share of the rent, a blessing since another baby, Letitia was born in 1816.

In 1817 John was transferred to a Pay Office of the Naval Yard at Chatham and had his outport supplement restored. The Dickenses moved into a three-story brick house on a hilltop at 2 Ordinance Place. The next five years were to be the happiest of Charles' young life. He never forgot the one time in his childhood when he felt loved and protected by his parents.

The Dickens family was fairly prosperous for a time. In spring, from his upstairs bedroom window, Charles could look across to a meadow ablaze with buttercups and daisies. Beyond he could see the dockyards and ships on the River Medway. Brother George and sister, Lucy lived in the next rooms. George had a wonderful magic lantern and Charles planned to marry Lucy (who was then six and had golden hair).

For his sixth birthday Lucy gave him a ring with a bit of red glass. Music echoed through the house, with Fanny playing the piano, John and Elizabeth singing, and Charles chiming in with them.

Abutting Chatham was the town of Rochester. A walk from one town into the other was like going from the modern world to the Middle Ages. Chatham was noisy, rowdy and littered with pubs and brothels. Whether or not Charles understood all he saw and heard at the time, his watchful eyes missed nothing. He remembered women in bright colors and clinking jewelry, busy marketplaces, pigtailed sailors, discharged soldiers with a stump for an arm or leg, and an old clothes shop he would transform into a place for David Copperfield to sell a jacket when he needed money.

In contrast, Rochester's ancient cathedral and castle ruin gave it dignity. Dickens returned to these places of his childhood often in his writing and in person for pleasure. The towns serve as the setting for his first novel, *Posthumous Papers of the Pickwick Club*. As Pickwick and the others drive past the old castle, his Mr. Jingle remarks in his jerky speech as if he had had the hiccups: "'Ah! fine place' said the stranger, 'glorious pile—frowning walls—tottering arches—dark nooks—crumbling staircases—Old cathedral, too—earthy smell—pilgrims' feet wor away the old steps—little Saxon doors ...'" Rochester's Bull's Inn on High Street appears in the novel when members of the Pickwick Club get rooms there.

In *The Mystery of Edwin Drood*, the book Dickens was writing when he died, Rochester is described as "[a] monotonous, silent city, deriving an earthy flavour throughout ..." One character, Grewgious, peers through the doors into the cathedral and mutters, "Dear me ... it's like looking down the throat of Old Time."

As a child, Charles thought of High Street as being as wide as a busy street in London, but on a visit years later found it to be "not much more than a lane." The town hall that he remembered as a "glorious structure" and one that he had imagined the Genie of the Lamp used as a model for Aladdin's palace was "a mere mean little heap of bricks." (Forster, 8)

Dickens often told friends of a walk he took with his father. Over the Rochester Bridge they strolled and up a slope to Gad's Hill Place to stare at a large brick house with bow windows and a small white bell turret on top of a gambrel (rounded) roof. A weather vane whirled on top of the turret. "... I can recollect my father, seeing me so fond of it, has often said to me, 'If you were persevering and were to work hard, you might some day come to live in it.'" (Forster, 6) (Charles would buy the house thirty-six years later.)

One of the Dickenses' servants, Mary Weller, told blood-curdling bedtime stories. She made ghoulish gestures, shrieked and moaned, and told of Captain Murdered who killed his wives, baked them into meat pies, and ate them. (A suspicious wife added poison to a pie that made the Captain swell to room-size and burst.) Mary's gory tales excited Charles' already vivid imagination and left him shivering, his blanket pulled over his head.

Did Dickens bring back to mind Mary's weird stories when he created the hateful Daniel Quilp of *The Old Curiosity Shop*? He wrote of the dwarf that "the grotesque expression of his face was a ghastly smile, which, ... constantly revealed the few discoloured fangs that were yet scattered in his mouth, and gave him the aspect of a panting dog."

Dickens also wrote of Quilp that "he ate hard eggs, shell and all, devoured giant prawns with head and tails on, chewed tobacco and watercresses at the same time ..." and "bit his fork and spoon until they bent ..."

Charles was a small, frail child. He suffered severe stomach pains that prevented him from joining in active games, but he was happy to sit with a book watching others play. His mother taught him to read. One day he found some tattered books in an upstairs room: *Tom Jones, Robinson Crusoe, Don Quixote, 1,001 Arabian Nights*, and *The Vicar of Wakefield*. He called the find "a glorious host, to keep me company" (Forster, 9) and played the hero in each book he read. "I have been Tom Jones (a child's Tom Jones, a harmless creature) for a week together," he said. (Forster, 10) Mary Weller called him "a terrible boy to read." (Johnson, 13) She recalled his spending hours reading his books and talking to the furniture in his room as he acted out the stories. He took flight on a magic carpet and explored the island of *Robinson Crusoe*.

Charles formed his lifelong fascination for the stage at the age of seven or eight, when John Dickens took him and Fanny to the theater. He loved the glitter, the gaslight, the unmistakable smell of the auditorium, and the clown who flopped and folded himself into various shapes; he even imitated the clown. Aunt Mary's friend James Lamert took Charles to Rochester's Theatre Royale to see several plays. The witches around the cauldron in Shakespeare's *Macbeth* worked their magic on Charles; at home he put on comedies and dramas he had composed for his sisters and friends.

With Fanny playing the piano, Charles sang in his clear, high treble voice, comical songs that he had learned. This delighted his father, who hoisted Charles onto a table to entertain guests. A favorite song was "The Cat's-Meat Man"; Charles sang the verses, and Fanny would come in on the chorus:

> Down in the street cries the cat's-meat man
> Fango, dango, with his barrow and can ....
> (Ackroyd, 63)

These days came to an abrupt end in 1821, when John Dickens' extravagance caught up with him and forced the growing family to leave Ordinance Terrace for a smaller house. Charles didn't mind the move, though; their new residence in St. Mary's Place, at the busy dockside end of Chatham, offered another exciting world for him to explore. Charles often walked beside his father to the Navy Pay Office, a two-story brick building in the heart of the port. While his father worked, Charles "watched the ropemakers and sniffed the smell of tarred rope, heard the anchorsmiths clanging away, saw the blockmakers surrounded by oak chips and wood shavings, and stood under the huge wooden walls of vessels rising in the slips, amid the exciting clatter and banging." (Johnson, 17)

Sometimes John would take him aboard the old yacht *Chatham* to sail up the Medway as far as the Thames, and "back in the dockyard once more, amid the canvas, and the clanging, and the booming, and the smell of oakum [hemp used for caulking seams] the boy would stare spell-bound at long files of convict laborers carrying planks of heavy timber, two tall men bearing all the weight and a little man in between ... happily carrying nothing." (Johnson, 17–18) Charles had always lived very near the ocean, excepting the short time in London, and he read sea stories, sang shanties, and would one day write of sailing adventures.

The house in St. Mary's Place was adjacent to a chapel, where Fanny and Charles attended a school run by William Giles, the minister's son. Charles excelled in his lessons, once winning a prize for a recitation. Wearing the same tall, white beaver hat as all the others, he felt like "one of the boys." They were known as "Giles' Cats," while other schools hosted "the Toy Town Rats" and "the Newrod Scrubbers."

In 1822, John Dickens was billeted back to London; he arranged for Charles to stay with Giles to finish the school term. The happy times in Chatham would be a bittersweet memory for Charles: no more climbing up to Gad's Hill Place to stare and dream; no more visits to the meadow, the Medway, the dockyard; no more meandering around Chatham and Rochester. Charles would always remember Mr. Giles fondly and treasure the schoolmaster's going-away present, a copy of Goldsmith's *Bee*.

THE DICKENS FAMILY RELOCATES

The stagecoach ride to London was lonely—"I consumed my sandwiches in solitude and dreariness, and it rained all the way, and I felt life was sloppier than I expected to find it." (Forster, 14)—but eventually he arrived at 16 Bayham Street, Camden Town. The large Dickens family, including the orphan maid and James Lamert as a boarder, squeezed into the four-room house. It had a basement, and its small rear attic was Charles' room. Off by himself in the attic, he felt abandoned, but his isolation was not the sole reason for it: Fanny had won a scholarship to the Royal Academy of Music, but despite his success at Giles' establishment, no mention was made of Charles' own schooling. Years later, Dickens wrote to John Forster, "I knew my father to be as kind and generous a man as lived in the world. Everything that I can remember of his conduct to his wife, or children, or friends ... is beyond all praise. But ... he appeared to have utterly lost at this time the idea of educating me at all, and to have utterly put from him the notion that I have any claim upon him in that regard whatever." (Forster, 16)

Debts piled up in the Dickens household, and Mrs. Dickens decided that she must do something about them. She believed that a school with paying pupils would bring in a tidy sum, so she found a larger house, on Gower Street, and had a brass plate inscribed *MRS. DICKENS ESTABLISHMENT* nailed to the front door. The venture was a failure from the start. There was no money to cover the rent for the larger house, the cost of the brass plate, or the handbills that Charles distributed throughout the neighborhood. And no pupils came—which was just as well, for Mrs. Dickens Establishment boasted neither furniture nor supplies.

Charles spent the days polishing his father's boots, caring for his siblings, and wandering about Camden Town. Two of his habitual excursions were pleasant ones: When he visited his uncle, Thomas

Barrow, he usually went home with an armful of books, for the Barrows' landlady, who owned a bookshop, would lend to Charles as many as he could carry. Other times he traveled to Limehouse, near the London docks, to see his godfather, Christopher Huffam, who made sails there. At Huffam's encouragement, Charles had the fun of putting on a performance of his comical songs for the old man's boatmaker friends. Visiting his godfather and seeing the Thames and the shipyards with their familiar sights, sounds, and smells was agreeably like being back in the Chatham dockyard. In general, though, Dickens, then eleven years old, seems to have lived through this period in poverty and loneliness and with an ardent and unfulfilled desire for education.

THE BLACKING FACTORY AND THE MARSHALSEA

The family continued to sink financially, and the situation became serious. A portion of John's salary went to pay off old debts. Those from whom he had borrowed would no longer lend. The baker and butcher banged on the door or shouted up to the window for payment. The time had come to pawn household goods, and since his father was working his mother sent Charles out to make the trade. His pride shattered, he slouched into pawn shops, timidly asking how much they would pay him; and he soon learned which shops would offer the best price. He developed a talent for it, a skill conspicuously absent from his later financial dealings; the sharp little boy would dicker with merchants over spoons or a lamp. He even had to sell his precious books, though he never parted with Giles' gift of Goldsmith's *Bee* and replaced the rest years later.

James Lamert, no longer their boarder, had gone into business as manager of a boot-blacking factory. James had been kind to Charles; he had taken him to theatrical performances and had even made for him a toy theater. Lamert suggested, with good intentions but to Charles' great distress, that the boy work at the factory, a plan to which John and Elizabeth Dickens agreed enthusiastically. Charles felt he was being cast aside once again. Two days after his twelfth birthday, Charles walked the three miles to Warren's Blacking, a factory that he would later describe as a "crazy tumble-down, old house abutting on the river ... literally overrun with rats" and "dirty and decayed." The "rotten floors and staircase," he would recall, "resounded with the squeaking and shuffling of the old grey rats swarming down in the cellars." (Forster, 25)

His job was "to cover the pots of paste blacking, first with a piece of oil-paper, and then with a bit of blue paper, to tie around with a string." (25) One of the boys, Bob Fagin, in a ragged apron and paper cap, showed Charles how to tie the string. After the tying, he must clip the paper neatly and paste on a label.

In his autobiography, Dickens underscored his humiliation: "No words can express the agony of my soul ... as I sunk into this companionship, compared these every day associates with those of my happier childhood, and felt my early hopes of growing up to be a learned and distinguished man, crushed in my breast." (26)

He hated the smell of the place, with its stenches of rotting wood, cement, and blacking corks. Furthermore, he detested his black-stained fingers, which repeated washings never managed to clean. In the squalid surroundings with the rats and dirt, the "common men and boys" of the workplace called him "the young gentleman," and Dickens too tried to think of himself in this way. (29) In spite of his misery, Dickens knew he would be criticized if he did not tie up as many pots as the others, so he pushed himself to show that he could work as fast as they did.

Two weeks after Dickens began his work at Warren's Blacking, John Dickens was arrested and imprisoned in the Marshalsea, a debtors' prison where inmates were permitted to have their families live with them. Fanny was still at school; Charles could not live in the prison, for he had a job, and as a result he had to board elsewhere. His mother found a room for him in Camden Town. The Navy continued to keep John on the payroll, perhaps out of sympathy for his five children. John had to pay the prison for his family's stay, but he did manage to contribute to the rent for the room Charles shared with two other boys. Charles would see his family on Sundays, when he met Fanny and together they went to dine at the prison.

The profoundly lonely twelve-year-old had been thrust out on his own to think and live as an adult. He looked forward to Saturday nights, when he would be paid and could walk about with money in his pocket. To make the bit of money last until Friday, he wrapped his weekly earnings of six shillings in six parcels, each labeled by day of the week. On the way to work in the morning, he passed pastry shops where the bakers sold day-old pastry at half-price. He was often tempted to buy something, and he sometimes did, but he knew that if he bought such a thing for breakfast then he could afford only a slice of pudding in the evening. The pudding he liked best was full of currants, but the portion was small for the price. At another shop, the pudding was "heavy and flabby" and the raisins few and far between, but he got more for his penny—many pudding suppers were had there. His situation was precarious: "I know that I lounged about the streets," he told John Forster, "insufficiently and unsatisfactorily fed. I know that, but for the mercy of God, I might have been, for any care that was taken of me, a little robber or a little vagabond." (Forster, 29–30)

Life in London streets with its sordid scenes and all manner of characters was Charles' education at that time. Images of it flood his work; in a novel he would write in 1855, Little Dorrit observes, "... London looks so large, so barren and so wild." (Dudgeon, 8)

The metropolis terrified and fascinated Dickens. It was the epicenter of thieving, wickedness, choking fog, abject poverty, and squalid prisons. He wandered past taverns, plodding horses pulling loaded wagons, shivering beggars, chimney sweeps, and men and women hawking a vast array of foods and other wares in the streets.

In spite of his dirty white beaver hat, shabby jacket, and corduroy breeches—or maybe because of them—Charles fantasized about a better life and tried occasionally to achieve some semblance of it. He once entered one of the finer dining rooms of Drury Lane with a paper-wrapped slice of bread tucked under his arm like a book. He ordered a small plate of beef from a waiter, who stared while Dickens ate; embarrassed, but trying to show some sophistication, Dickens gave the waiter a halfpenny tip, which he later sincerely wished the waiter had refused.

Dickens realized there was no escape from his job at Warren's Blacking, and the pressures of living alone, missing his family, and scrounging for food often had him in tears. When he begged his father for help, John arranged for a room near the Marshalsea, close enough for his son to have breakfast and supper with the family every day, "at home." Although the room was a back attic with a mattress on the floor, Charles called it "paradise." (Forster, 31) He arrived daily before the prison gates opened, and while waiting he studied the others in attendance—"[s]uch threadbare coats, such squashed hats and bonnets" (Ackroyd, 173)—contemplating their occupations, their residences, the conditions of their lives. The man who would become a master of characterization locked these people, in all their variety, into his memory—clothes, headgear, dirty hands, laughter, and all. During the time spent in the prison, Dickens observed the activity there and the occupants so intently that had he been an artist his drawings would have included the every minute detail.

After work each day, he returned for supper and stayed until nine o'clock, when he plodded back to his dark "paradise." His father's prison tales gave the future author fodder for flights of imagination while he covered his blacking pots.

Three months into John Dickens' imprisonment, an inheritance from his mother's estate enabled him to pay off his most pressing creditors and gain the family's release from the Marshalsea. Mrs. Dickens found a house in a rundown section of Camden Town, but neither parent said a word about Charles' leaving the factory.

DICKENS RETURNS TO SCHOOL

In the blacking factory's new quarters in Covent Garden, Charles and Bob Fagin worked next to a window where passersby could see them. The boy's dexterity in covering, pasting, and tying up many pots inside of a few minutes attracted a crowd. Enraged at seeing his son on exhibition, John sent Lamert a letter of complaint, but Lamert resented John's attitude in view of all he had done for the family. He fired Charles straightaway, but Mrs. Dickens would not hear of it—she insisted they needed Charles' seven shillings a week. Whether John was prompted by pride or by a genuine desire to be of use to his clever son, he refused to grovel to Lamert: the boy would go to school. For Charles, this was salvation; he would not bring the experience of the blacking factory back to life—in his memory or in his fiction—until he wrote of Mr. Murdstone's sending David to the bottling warehouse in *David Copperfield*. It pained Charles at the time that his parents could not agree on his future, and twenty years later he would still remember his impression of it: "... I never shall forget, I never can forget that my mother was warm for me being sent back." (Johnson, 44)

In late June of 1824, delighted to be a pupil again, Charles entered Wellington House Academy. His classmates would not have believed this neatly dressed, happy-go-lucky fellow had recently roamed the streets; to them, he was just a short, handsome boy who smiled often and held his head high, perhaps to appear taller.

Remembering the school in later years, Charles would call William Jones, the headmaster, "by far the most ignorant man I have ever had the pleasure to know." (MacKenzie, 18) He kept a "bloated mahogany ruler" handy that he used on the boys' palms or "viciously drawing a pair of pantaloons tight with one of his large hands and caning the wearer with the other." (Johnson, 49) Charles managed to stay clear of the ruler most of the time.

One of the masters taught math, English, writing, mended the pens, and called on the parents. The deaf Latin master stuck onions in his ears in hopes of helping his deafness and the little fat dancing master taught them "The sailor's Hornpipe." Mr. Jones went about brandishing his "bloated mahogany ruler."

Academics seemed to place second to the training of white mice, harboring bees, other small animals, and birds that the boys kept in hatboxes and desks. One white mouse living in the cover of a Latin dictionary could pull small Roman chariots that the boys made and appeared in one of their plays, *The Dog of Montagis*, in the title role. They lost him to an inkwell when he fell in and drowned.

At the school, Charles was once more a boy among boys and described by a schoolmate as a mischief-maker. With a group of chums he went along the street asking passersby for money, especially old ladies, who would often say that "they had no money for beggar boys." (Forster, 49) Roaring with laughter, the boys would race off.

When Charles had a penny, he bought *The Terrific Register*, a penny-weekly. Every issue would have one illustration, "in which there was always a pool of blood and at least one body." He said it was worth a penny for "making myself unspeakably miserable and frightening my very wits out of my head." (Forster, 48)

DICKENS RETURNS TO WORK

Just past his fifteenth birthday, Charles had to leave school, again because of the family's finances. John and Elizabeth Dickens now had the added expense of a sixth child, Augustus, and, unable to pay the house rent, they were evicted. Mrs. Dickens wasted no time in seeing to it that Charles brought home a salary. She secured a position for him as clerk in the law firm of Ellis and Blackmore. Work at the firm was dull for Charles—carrying bundles of papers from law offices to court, serving processes, and keeping the petty cash ledger.

When time dragged, Dickens would carve his initials on his desk top or fling cherry pits out of the second story window on people in the street below. If someone complained, he—with a look of innocence on his boyish face—would say they must be mistaken. Mainly, he watched, listened, and absorbed, making mental notes of the office workers: Mr. Ellis, a snuff-sniffer, forever pulling out his snuffbox, would appear as Mr. Perker in *The Pickwick Papers*; the eccentric Newman Knott would become Newman Noggs in *Nicholas Nickleby*.

One of Dickens' *Sketches by Boz*, "Making a Night of It," mentions the evenings spent with a fellow clerk, Thomas Potter. They were "thick and thin" pals, and, after dining on "chops and kidneys with a draught of stout," they would sample mild Havana cigars and Scotch with water and then attend performances at low-priced theaters, where admission was one shilling in the galleries (the top balconies) and after nine o'clock they could see the show at half-price.

George Lear, another colleague at Ellis and Blackmore, remarked that he thought he knew the London streets quite well but learned that he knew almost nothing in comparison with young Dickens. Dickens knew not only the streets by heart, but also the people. "He could imitate in a manner that I never heard equaled," Lear later testified, "the low population of the streets of London in all their varieties whether mere loafers or sellers of fruit, vegetables, or anything else. Besides these, he could impersonate all the leading actors and popular singers of the day, comic or patriotic." (Johnson, 55)

The evenings were fun, but the days at Ellis and Blackmore were boring. If he remained there as a clerk, he might—with considerable patience and study—become a wealthy solicitor or even a judge; but in his opinion law was slow and "humbug." He wanted to climb the ladder of success more quickly.

John Dickens shared his son's ambition. To improve the family's situation, the elder Dickens decided to become a newspaper reporter; in Chatham he'd gained some experience from writing a two-column account of a fire. He began the difficult task of learning shorthand and, surprisingly, accomplished this in a year. *The British Press* hired him as a Parliamentary reporter. The fifteen guineas John Dickens earned compared to Charles' own fifteen shillings a week, gave Charles pause; he began to consider a career in journalism. He was confident that he could learn shorthand, and a newspaper office seemed more exciting than a law office. (While at Wellington House Academy, Charles too had submitted reports of fires and accidents to *The British Press*, who had paid a penny per printed line.)

Charles spent a half-guinea for a book that claimed to be an easy way to learn shorthand, which proved notoriously difficult. He doggedly attacked the study of dots that in one position meant one thing and in another meant something else. He said the squiggly lines like "flies' legs" and some like parts of cobwebs "... not only troubled my waking hours, but reappeared before me in my sleep. When I fixed these wretches in my mind, I found they had driven everything else out of it." Dickens later put David Copperfield through the same torture: David "plunges onto a sea of perplexity" and laments, "[W]hen I had groped my way, blindly, through these difficulties, and had mastered the alphabet, which was an Egyptian Temple in itself, there then appeared a procession of new horrors."

Dickens left Ellis and Blackmore in November of 1828. He practiced his shorthand and developed such speed and accuracy that he would be praised later as "the best shorthand reporter in Parliament." (Forster, 55) Not quite seventeen, he was yet too young for the press gallery of the House of Commons. A relative who was a freelance reporter in the Consistory Court of Doctors' Commons let Charles sit in the box in which the reporters waited until called upon to transcribe a case. David Copperfield is told that Doctors' Commons, several different courts that met in the same hall, is "a place that has an ancient monopoly in suits about peoples' wills, and peoples' marriages, and disputes about ships and boats."

Soon Dickens was able to rent his own box, working principally for the Consistory Court that handled cases pertaining to the Church. He once was called upon to transcribe a case involving quarrels in a church vestry. The task required many unnecessary pages of transcript, and Dickens was impatient with, and scornful of, the pompous attorneys whose archaic modes of expending time and money he believed an obstruction of justice. He would later write the absurdity of the case into *Sketches by Boz*, naming the litigants Bumpls and Sludberry.

To celebrate his eighteenth birthday, he obtained a reader's ticket to the British Museum. For admittance to the upstairs Reading Room he had to pull a bell cord to summon an attendant to check him in. He pored over works of Shakespeare, Goldsmith's *History of England*, and any other books that might advance his program of self-education. He also joined a circulating library, where he borrowed books of the macabre, a taste that might date to the scary stories he had heard from Mary Weller. (He incorporated the bizarre and macabre into another

Boz sketch, the morbid "The Black Veil," a gothic tale of imprisonment
and madness involving a troubled hangman and his good mother.)

THE BEADNELL AFFAIR; GROWTH AS A REPORTER

Dickens found law reporting to be a monotonous way to make a living
that didn't guarantee a steady source of income when the courts were out
of session. Too, he was madly in love with Maria Beadnell, a ravishing
beauty with bright eyes and dark curls who was of just his height. He
didn't expect her father, a wealthy banker, to accept an impoverished
shorthand reporter as his son-in-law. He needed prosperity, and he
needed it to come quickly.

To make money and "a great splash" (MacKenzie, 24), Dickens
seriously considered a career as an actor. He did not doubt his acting
ability and was a good comic singer. For three years he had spent night
after night in theaters, studying the actors' expressions and movements.
At home, he'd practiced scenes from plays he'd memorized, complete
with gestures and poses, entrances and exits. He now went so far as to
write to the stage manager of the Lyceum Theater to request an
audition. (He was called back, but a bad cold kept him from keeping the
appointment.) In the meantime, an uncle, John Barrow, offered him a
job that Dickens had been hoping for: *The Mirror of Parliament*, a weekly
journal that Barrow owned, reported on business carried on in the
House of Lords and the House of Commons, and Dickens became a
parliamentary reporter.

Dickens believed he was making headway with his career, but was
not so sure about Maria. She could be flirtatious and had him in turmoil,
but she was his angel, and he felt he could die for her. He dreamed of
Maria as his wife. They exchanged letters and gifts, and Dickens believed
that she loved him. Mr. and Mrs. Beadnell were friendly at first and
welcomed Dickens into their home, but they soon began to wonder
about this young man, whose family background and social position
were not at all to their standard. Mr. Beadnell learned that John Dickens
had been in the Marshalsea and decided Maria should go away to school
in Paris to forget her "Mr. Dickin." How he would live without seeing
her he did not know, but for part of the time at least he had to
concentrate on reporting. He now had a second job on the staff of a new
evening paper, *The True Sun*.

At the time, the House of Commons made no special accommodation for newspapermen, who had to crowd into the back row of the poorly ventilated Stranger's Gallery, where it was difficult to hear and too dark to read. "I have worn my knees," Dickens said, "by writing on them in the old [gallery] of the old House of Commons, and I have worn my feet by standing to write in a preposterous pen in the old House of Lords where we used to be huddled together like so many sheep." (Forster, 61)

Most days, he yawned with boredom at the empty political rhetoric that he had to transcribe, though there were notable exceptions. Once the Irish leader O'Connell spoke against a bill for "suppression of disturbances" in Ireland. He gave a dramatic picture of a poor widow looking for her son among the bodies of peasants killed by soldiers; Dickens set down his pencil and wept.

At the end of July of 1832, Dickens resigned from the left-wing *The True Sun*, at a time when the paper was in danger of going under. He had advanced to a position of sub-editor at *The Mirror of Parliament*.

Dickens was called upon to take down the first part of an address that continued to run long enough to require the coverage of eight reporters. He took down the end of the speech. The Chief Secretary for Ireland asked for the reporter who had transcribed the first and last parts of the address, as the rest was full of errors and must be rewritten. When Dickens entered, the man saw a short, bright-eyed, boyish-looking young man with wavy, shoulder-length brown hair. The Irish secretary said he had asked for the *gentleman* who had reported his speech.

"I am that gentleman," Dickens answered. (Johnson, 55) With a slight frown and hint of a smile, the secretary offered a chair at the desk, but the reporter said that he was used to writing on his knees.

Dickens was fast becoming man of distinction among reporters and had an important role in running the paper, but his love affair with Maria Beadnell was going nowhere. Maria returned to England, but her attitude toward him had become cold and unfriendly. After an exchange of several letters—his of fervent love, hers indifferent—he gave up and finally wrote to her, "I have borne more from you than I do believe any creature breathing ever bore from a woman before." (Johnson, 79) He returned all her gifts and letters with a note saying that it would be mean of him to keep a gift or even a word of her affection and that he could "only wish that I could as easily forget that I ever received them." (Johnson, 75)

Years later he told Forster that his love had "excluded every other idea from my mind for four years." Still, he seems to have gotten over it: "I have positively stood amazed at myself," he said to Forster, "ever since." His love for Maria had inspired him "with determination to overcome all differences which finally lifted me up into that newspaper life." (Ackroyd, 131)

And the inspiration must have stayed with him, for Dickens turned to serious writing during Parliament's recess. He wrote his first short story, "Dinner at Poplar Walk," in 1833. "With fear and trembling," he said, he dropped the story "into the dark letter-box in a dark office up a dark court in Fleet Street" (Johnson, 91), the home of *Monthly Magazine*. A few weeks later, he bought the magazine and perused it— and found himself a published author. "I walked down to Westminster Hall and turned into it for half an hour, because my eyes so dimmed with joy and pride that they could not bear the street, and were not fit to be seen there." (Johnson, 92)

The editor of *Monthly Magazine* asked for more. Dickens sent in a story each month, for which he received no pay and, until August, no byline. For the August issue he began to use the pseudonym "Boz," his youngest brother's nickname.

Dickens' eyes were like a camera. His sketches captured full-blown pictures of the comedy and pathos of London street life. Walking the London streets after a day's work at Warren's Blacking had been his only amusement. In later years he considered a brisk walk of thirty miles an evening's entertainment. His daughter Kate recalled, "[H]e would walk through the busy, noisy streets which would act on him like a tonic and enable him to take up with new vigor the flagging interest of his story and breathe new life into its pages." (Schwarzbach, 27) He wrote of Seven Dials, a maze of courts, lanes, and alleys, of pawnbroker's shops, and of hackney coaches' horses with drooping heads and scant manes. One sketch by Boz, "The Streets—Morning," told of "Covent Garden market ... thronged with carts of all sorts [and] sizes ... from the heavy lumbering wagon with its four stout horses to the jingling costermonger's cart with its consumptive donkey. The pavement is already strewed with decayed cabbage leaves ... men are shouting ... basket women talking ... donkeys braying." In another sketch, "The Streets—Night," "the baked potato man has departed—the kidney pie man has just walked away with his warehouse on his arm—the cheesemonger has drawn in his blind."

For some time, Dickens had hoped to be hired as a reporter for *The Morning Chronicle*, a liberal newspaper (he had no love for the Tories). In 1834 he achieved that goal when his friend Thomas Beard recommended Dickens for the job as "the fastest and most accurate man in the gallery." (Johnson, 93) He celebrated the prospect of receiving a steady salary for the first time in his life, of putting behind him the shame of his days as a shabbily dressed blacking warehouse "slave" with dirty fingernails. Those days had left him with an obsession with cleanliness and neatness. Always smartly but conservatively dressed, he shocked his friends by turning out in fancy waistcoats and an elegant cape with velvet trim.

During Parliamentary recesses, *The Morning Chronicle* might send him anywhere to report on political speeches, dinners, or public meetings. The excitement of traveling—he'd never been very far from London and the South of England—and rushing back at midnight to deliver his copy was an experience the energetic and restless Dickens loved. Rivalry between *The Morning Chronicle* and *The Times* made it even more exciting. Journalists raced each other back to the city to be first in with a story.

Dickens told that he had "often transcribed for the printer from my shorthand reports ... writing on the palm of my hand, by the light of a dark lantern, in a post chaise and four, galloping through a wild country, all in the dead of night." (Johnson, 155) He said they could be forty or fifty miles from London in a rickety carriage with exhausted horses and drunken postboys and still return in time for publication.

The ride back to London was often long and perilous. During a downpour, mud would splash up into the coach window. Dickens, who hated dirt, had to wipe mud off his face and papers. Sometimes coach wheels got stuck in mud or even came off. Still, in spite of the hazards and the demand for speed and absolute accuracy, Dickens reveled in the thrill of it. "There never was anybody connected with news-papers," he said, "who, in the same space of time, had so much express and post-chaise experience as I." (Johnson, 193) He told of a time he took down an election speech "... under such a pelting rain that I remember two good-natured colleagues held a pocket handkerchief over my notebook." (Ackroyd, 155)

Besides the traveling and writing London street sketches for the *Chronicle*, the paper sent him out to do theater reviews. At one play he found he was reviewing his own sketch, "Bloomsburg Christening," although the program gave the author as "J.B. Buckstone."

Then, just as he was getting ahead financially, Dickens had to bail out his father once again; John Dickens had been arrested for non-payment of a wine merchant's bill. He paid off his father's debts and found cheaper lodgings for his mother and his siblings, but he had to borrow to pay the £35 rent for his rooms at Furnival's Inn. With no funds left with which to furnish his bare new quarters, he had to make do with a table, two or three chairs, and some books, since he had "*no dishes*, no curtains, and no french polish." (MacKenzie, 28)

CATHERINE HOGARTH; THE SUCCESS OF BOZ

George Hogarth, a friendly, unconventional Scot, had been a lawyer, then a journalist in Edinburgh, then the music critic for *The Morning Chronicle*, and now had been appointed editor of the new *Evening Chronicle*. He asked Dickens to contribute a series of his street sketches to the paper, which printed twenty sketches over the next seven months—to add several guineas to his weekly salary.

Impressed with the young author, Hogarth invited Dickens into his home to meet his family of three daughters and seven sons. Dickens enjoyed the company of the family, and in particular the three daughters. Catherine, the oldest, was nineteen, Mary fourteen, and Georgina seven. Catherine was pretty, and her large, heavy-lidded eyes gave her a captivating and languid voluptuousness. Dickens' enjoyment of her company became first a marked preference and then love. This courtship proved nothing like his earlier infatuation with Maria for he had learned not to love blindly, nor to be used. He wanted a woman in whose world he would be the center, whose feelings and actions would revolve around his needs. The two became engaged in 1835.

Catherine did not have Maria Beadnell's flirtatious ways, and he soon realized that she could be petulant and sulky. After an argument, Dickens wrote her, "[d]earest darling Pig," and "my Dearest Life," and "God bless you, my dearest Girl." (Johnson, 125) He admonished her in kindly but stern words indicating he would brook no defiance from her. He warned that he was not to be trifled with, and that if she tired of him she must say so. Fearing she must be at fault, she wrote asking his forgiveness and begging him to love her again. He answered, "I have never ceased to love you for one moment since I knew you, nor shall I." (Johnson, 124)

Soon thereafter, Catherine and her mother both caught scarlet fever. Dickens sent affectionate letters, lines of kisses, and a copy of William Harrison Ainsworth's popular novel *Rookwood*.

Dickens had met Ainsworth himself at the *Chronicle* office in 1835. He admired the flamboyant novelist and imitated him, even to the point of affecting his flashy style of waistcoats and gold rings. Ainsworth at first was his model and mentor, but he later became a rival. At that time Dickens was still a struggling parliamentary reporter, but Londoners were already calling him "Boz the Magnificent"—and "Have you read Boz?" was a frequent question at social gatherings, the understanding being that one *had*. Ainsworth was taken with Dickens' enthusiasm and wit and invited him to join his circle of writers and artists. Dickens would become fast friends with the writer Thomas Carlyle, the artist and novelist William Makepeace Thackeray, the well-known cartoonist George Cruikshank, the esteemed editor and novelist Edward Bulwer-Lytton, and the writer Benjamin Disraeli, who would become Britain's prime minister in 1868.

Dickens also met John Macrone, Ainsworth's publisher. Excited about the *Sketches*, Macrone said they were "capital value" and should be published in book form. He made an offer of £150 for the copyright to the first edition. Dickens was to write enough sketches to fill two volumes, and the publisher would commission Cruikshank to illustrate. Dickens was thrilled with the offer and honored to be working with "Illustrious George," whose knowledge of London streets rivaled his own. He was bursting with ideas of gin shops, ladies' societies, omnibuses, a Parliament sketch, and a sketch of Newgate Prison, where condemned men spent their last night. Dickens planned to visit—a look inside would be necessary to fully describe the gruesome sights of this prison that was more terrifying than the Marshalsea. Macrone suggested the title for the book, *Bubbles from the Brain of Boz*, but Dickens preferred the simpler *Sketches by Boz*.

In November of 1835, Dickens, still reporting, rushed with Thomas Beard from one election to another. For their journey to Bristol, Dickens suggested they would make better time on horseback than the *Times* boys, who would travel by coach. Dickens and Beard had to cover a speech one day and a dinner the following night; by staying up and writing for two nights, they made the next morning's edition, and scooped *The Times*.

The editor of *Bell's Life in London* asked for Boz sketches. Dickens wrote a series of twelve, entitled *Scenes and Characters* and met with Cruikshank to discuss illustrations. Then, John Hullah, a composer friend of Fanny's from the Academy of Music, asked Dickens to write the libretto for his operetta *The Gondolier*. Characteristically, Dickens insisted on changing the setting from the canals of Venice to the byways of England. Hullah felt forced to give in, and Dickens renamed the piece *The Village Coquettes*. (This was not the only instance of Dickens' revising the work of others to suit his own vision.)

In addition to his reporting commitments, he wrote more Boz sketches for Macrone. When Catherine complained that Charles was too busy to see her, he replied that his work was for her, for "a home for both of us." He said, "I can never write with effect ... until I have got my steam up ... until I have become so excited with my subject that I cannot leave off." (MacKenzie, 37) He made his apologies with the wish that he could be with her. In anticipation of the wedding, Dickens reserved larger and brighter rooms at Furnival's Inn, rooms that would not be available until February 15.

Sketches by Boz was released on the author's twenty-fourth birthday, February 7, 1836, to rave reviews—even *The Times* praised it. In his review in *The Evening Chronicle*, Hogarth compared "A Visit to Newgate" to Victor Hugo's work. He credited Boz "with a strong sense of the ridiculous and a graphic faculty of placing in the most whimsical and amusing lights the follies and absurdities of human nature. He has the power, too, of producing tears as well as laughter." (Johnson, 109)

THE SUCCESS OF THE PICKWICK PAPERS

William Hall, of the publishing firm of Chapman and Hall, appeared at Dickens' apartment with an offer: Dickens was to write a few lines as captions to drawings by comic artist Richard Seymour. The drawings were of members of the Nimrod Club going fishing and shooting, sports at which they were inept. Dickens agreed to Hall's offer, but on his own terms: He said he was "no great sportsman except in regards to all kinds of locomotion" (Forster, 68) and that the idea had been done several times before. He thought the illustrations should come out of the text rather than the reverse. Richard Seymour was nervous and given to spells of depression, and he flew into a rage when he heard the arrangement. The "hack" who was to write but a few lines had taken over his idea and relegated him to second place. Nevertheless, having no other work in the offing, he acquiesced to the arrangement.

Hall suggested that the book be published in monthly installments with the expectation of profiting twice, first from the magazine sales and later from book royalties. Dickens notified Chapman and Hall that he was well into the first chapter of *The Posthumous Papers of the Pickwick Club*, with all the members of the club represented: Samuel Pickwick, whose exact description was still up for debate; Augustus Snodgrass, the resident poet; Tracy Tupman, with an eye for the ladies; and Nathaniel Winkle, afraid of horses and on dangerous and unfriendly terms with a gun. Dickens included the clumsy Mr. Winkle in deference to the artist, who had already sketched the character trying to shoot a bird. The name *Pickwick* he appropriated from Moses Pickwick, the owner of a fleet of coaches. The first number of *Pickwick* was to appear on March 31, 1836. Along with finishing other work, Dickens had to have the second installment ready at the time of the publication of the first. He told Catherine he had trouble keeping his mind on it—the excitement of their wedding, to be held on April 2, made concentration difficult.

He met his deadline and made it to the church on time. Thomas Beard, his best man, spoke of the ceremony as "a very quiet piece of business." (MacKenzie, 43) After a wedding breakfast at the Hogarth home, Charles took his bride for a week's honeymoon to a cottage a few miles from Rochester, the beloved countryside of his boyhood. They returned to live for a time in Furnival's Inn, to which rooms their mothers had added homey touches with a recovered sofa and Charles' indifferent brown beer mugs arranged on a shelf.

Expecting *Pickwick* to be comical, its reviewers found it "excessively dull." (Johnson, 135) Sales lagged; the first installments did not repeat the success of *Sketches by Boz*. Richard Seymour had drawn Pickwick as tall and thin, when author and publishers had wanted him to be portly. Dickens described for Seymour "a fat old beau who would wear ... drab tights and black gaiters." (Johnson, 119) Seymour seized the idea at last and created the now-familiar plump, bespectacled Samuel Pickwick.

Dickens complimented Seymour on his revised depiction of Pickwick, but he said the illustration for another scene was not *quite* right and explained exactly what he wanted. Seymour reworked the drawing; upon completing it, the chronically depressed man took his own life, spelling disaster for the publication. On top of this personal tragedy, the first four chapters of *Pickwick* did not sell. The publishers now were losing money *and* had lost the artist whose name had given clout to the enterprise. Despite the setbacks, Dickens had confidence in his ability to save *Pickwick*. He had just offered to write eight extra pages to make up for the lack of illustrations when hope appeared, in the form of the artist Hablot Knight Browne. The publishers were pleased with Browne's work, and Dickens liked the shy young illustrator, nicknamed "Phiz," with whom he embarked on a partnership that would span twenty-three years.

Still, sales of *Pickwick* did not pick up until the episode in which Mr. Pickwick discovers the droll Sam Weller cleaning boots in the yard of the White Hart Inn and hires Weller as his servant. Weller added the folksy, idiosyncratic humor that readers loved. (With the Pickwick members off on a shooting jaunt, Sam creates a "Wellerism" as he removes a veal pie from the picnic basket: "Wery good thing is weal pie when you know the lady as made it, and is sure it ain't kittens." He goes on to tell of a pieman who owned cats: "'They're all made o' them noble animals,' says he, a pointin' to a wery nice little tabby kitten, 'and I seasons 'em for beef-steak, weal, or kidney, 'cordin' to the demand.'") Dickens found his pace when Weller, with his Cockney wisdom, entered the story. Pickwick evolved from a humorous, gullible character into a noble, benevolent man. Weller calls him "an angel in gaiters."

Ever the journalist, Dickens showed his opinion of British law as contemptible and comic in the series, too, during Pickwick's suit for breach of promise, brought to trial by his landlady. Dickens painted the scene in which Pickwick finds himself in debtors' prison for refusing to pay unjust damages from his memory of his father's time in the Marshalsea.

Although *Pickwick* had very little plot, and was essentially a rambling account of the characters' adventures and encounters along the way, the public bought 40,000 copies every month. Pickwick hats and canes appeared, as did a *Sam Weller's Pickwick Jest Book*. In 1836 Dickens wrote Chapman and Hall, "If I live to be a hundred years and write three novels in each, I should never be so proud as I am of *Pickwick*." (Johnson, 156)

JOHN FORSTER; THE TRIALS OF SUCCESS;
THE DEATH OF MARY HOGARTH

Within a few months, Dickens' life came into full bloom, with his marriage, the success of *Pickwick*, his reputation as Boz, and his approaching fatherhood. He continued at his usual breakneck pace, revising *The Village Coquettes* for a December opening, rewriting one of his sketches ("The Great Winglebury Duel") as a play, which he re-titled *The Strange Gentleman*, turning out chapters for *Pickwick*, and cantering over muddy roads on reporting assignments.

For several weeks *The Village Coquettes* had been undergoing rewrites of the lyrics and Hullah's music. On July 23, 1836 a group gathered in Furnival's Inn to hear Dickens read the play and to listen to the score. John Braham, the tenor who would sing the lead, was enthusiastic. The stage manager of the St. James Theater said, "Bet you it runs fifty nights." (Johnson, 148) *The Strange Gentleman* opened at the theater in September and played for *sixty* nights.

The success of *Pickwick* and the *Sketches* generated more offers of work than Dickens could handle, but he gladly accepted them. In October, Richard Bentley, owner of a new magazine styled *Bentley's Miscellany*, made him a lucrative offer to serve as editor and to include sixteen pages of his own writing each month at seventy-five percent more money than Chapman and Hall were paying him for *Pickwick*. With this handsome increase in his income, he would be able, safely, to leave his job with *The Morning Chronicle*.

On Christmas Day in 1836, Dickens met John Forster—who would become a major force in his life and in the history of Dickens criticism—at Richard Ainsworth's home. Forster had a background in law, but he had found law as distasteful as Dickens had found it. His interests had turned to literature and theater. Thackeray once said of Forster, "Whenever anybody is in a scrape we all fly to him for refuge— he is omniscient and works miracles." (Johnson, 187) Robert Browning thought Forster "laughed like a rhinoceros," and Thomas Carlyle found him "a most noisy man." (MacKenzie, 53) In any case, Forster gave generously of his time, effort, and expertise to writers whose work he admired. His first impression of Dickens was that he looked extremely youthful, with no whiskers whatsoever and a great deal of rich brown hair. The young author gave him the sense that he did not hold back any opinions; Dickens seemed to him a man of action, with an eager, energetic outlook. Forster—opinionated, overbearing, and often quarrelsome—recognized Dickens' inability to tend to his own affairs and intervened. He would become the author's literary agent, proofreader, critic, and biographer, and the two would remain the closest of friends throughout Dickens' life.

For Dickens, the association with Forster was lifesaving. Fame had come too quickly for Dickens, and his commitments were a tangled mess. His talent was abundant, but he lacked a sense of how to market his work—and he had never learned to curb his impulsiveness. He accepted all offers that came his way and at too low a price, for a paradoxical lack of self-confidence made him underestimate his value as a writer. Indeed, Dickens had written for *Monthly Magazine* without any pay at all. Thinking of himself as a mere reporter, when John Macrone had offered to publish the *Sketches* in book form, Dickens had been so excited by the prospect of seeing his work in a book that he had signed over the copyright for a mere £150. Furthermore, he had agreed to only £200 for the copyright of a novel—*Gabriel Vardon, Locksmith of London*— that he had promised to deliver by November of 1836. Chapman and Hall had then approached him with an offer for *Pickwick*, and soon thereafter Richard Bentley had appeared with the request to edit *Bentley's Miscellany*. Bentley had offered to buy two novels for £500 each. When Macrone had heard that Dickens had signed with Bentley, he'd insisted on completion of *Gabriel Vardon*. Dickens had persuaded Macrone to withdraw his demand for *Vardon* by selling him the copyright to the *Sketches* for £250. His need for a cool head like Forster's was obvious and urgent.

Still, because he was busy overseeing rehearsals for *The Village Coquettes*, meeting the increased page requirements of *Pickwick*, working on Bentley's magazine, and beginning *Oliver Twist* for the *Miscellany's* February issue, Dickens—though he desperately needed Forster's help— did not see his new friend again for two months. But things were not going at all badly; Dickens' son was born on January 6, 1837, and the first issue of *Bentley's Miscellany* came out a few days before that. The child was named Charles Culliford ("Charley"), and the magazine sold in the thousands.

Catherine slipped into a depression after the birth of Charley, and her sister Mary Hogarth, then about seventeen, took up residence with her sister and brother-in-law to tend to the household. With the two new additions, the living quarters in Furnival's Inn became too crowded for Dickens' growing family; he found a new residence at 48 Doughty Street, on a private lane. The building came complete with a porter, dressed in a uniform and a gold-laced hat, who closed the gates at night.

More trouble with Macrone brought Forster to Dickens' aid. Now that he owned the rights, Macrone planned to publish the *Sketches* in monthly installments. Dickens could not accept Macrone's making thousands from a copyright sold in haste. When Forster consulted Macrone about selling back the copyright, the latter asked for £2,000. At that price, Forster advised Dickens to keep quiet for a time; the impatient Dickens could not.

Chapman and Hall decided it would be to their advantage to buy, with Dickens, the copyright to *Sketches* for £2,250, deducting Dickens' share from the profits. Without consulting Forster, Dickens agreed to the transaction. When he asked Forster, "Was I right?" his friend said that he "was glad to have been no party to a price so exorbitant." (Johnson, 200)

After that episode, Forster took over. In view of the increase in popularity of the author's works he made a settlement with Bentley to pay Dickens £700 for *Barnaby Rudge*, formerly titled *Gabriel Vardon*. He proofread all work before it went out, beginning with the fifteenth number of *Pickwick*. Besides Forster's help in clearing his desk, Dickens now had a companion to accompany him on long walks and horseback rides.

The large Doughty Street house was a comfortable, roomy setting in which to entertain Dickens' guests and extended family in style. Good cheer and laughter rang through the house. Frederick, gifted as his father, entertained with comical imitations. Dickens and Mary Hogarth had a clear mutual admiration for each other. Dickens thought of sweet, lighthearted Mary as domestic perfection in a young woman, and she too adored *him*.

But the joy of the relationship soon gave way to grief. After midnight on May 7, 1837—just after the three Dickenses' attendance at a production of Charles' recently completed comic burletta, *Is She His Wife?*—Mary collapsed with a heart attack; she died in her brother-in-law's arms on the following day. Dickens was shattered. He poured out his heart in letters to friends expressing his love for her and wrote, " ... she has been the grace and life of our home—the admired of all for her beauty and excellence." He said, "I have lost the dearest friend I ever had." (Johnson, 196, 199) Indeed, Dickens would keep her clothing, revisiting it periodically in the years to come.

The epitaph he composed for Mary read: "Young, beautiful and good, God in His Mercy numbered her with his angels at the early age of seventeen." (Johnson, 197) He had slipped a ring from her finger and put it on his own, to wear the rest of his life.

For the first time in his writing career Dickens found himself unable to work. He had notices printed explaining the reason. There would be no numbers of *Pickwick Papers* or *Oliver Twist* during that month of mourning; this is the only known instance of his missing a deadline on an accepted commission.

Mary came to him in dreams for a long time afterward. The girls in his novels all revealed something of Mary: Rose Maylie in *Oliver Twist*, Ada Clare in *Bleak House*, and especially Little Nell in *The Old Curiosity Shop*, whose death scene he wept to write.

THE AFTERMATH

To give time to recover from shock and to rest, Dickens and Catherine spent the next two weeks in the quiet of a country farm. Returning to Doughty Street, Dickens made an effort to recollect his energies. He had difficulty in finding a pace for *Oliver Twist*. Writing about the rejected child in the workhouse brought to mind the nightmarish times in the blacking warehouse, and Dickens put Oliver through even more frightening miseries than he himself had experienced. Thoughts of the poor boy depressed Dickens, even making him feel physically ill. He said that he was "suffering a violent attack of God knows what, in the head." (MacKenzie, 56)

Oliver Twist was a condemnation of the Poor Law Amendment Act. Because of starvation wages the law forced people to live in workhouses where they received little food. They had the choice of starving to death either slowly in the workhouse or more quickly on the outside. The law tore families apart, for females lived in one section of the workhouse and males in another—and in the novel, Oliver Twist discovers that the answer to a request for more food is a beating and imprisonment in the dark. Some readers objected to the book's exposure of the evils of the Poor Law; others did not want to face up to the squalid conditions existing in their city.

Dickens wrote simultaneously the final installments of Pickwick's humorous adventures and the desperate plight of Oliver Twist, during which time John Dickens was causing still more trouble. With Charles making money for Chapman and Hall, John took it upon himself to borrow against his son's good name until he owed a large sum, not only to the publishers, but also to tradesmen. Again he faced debtors' prison, and again Charles paid the debts. To get his parents out of town and away from the temptation to borrow, he rented and furnished a small country house for them.

In June of 1837, after a performance of *Othello*, John Forster introduced Dickens to the Shakespearean actor William Macready. Macready had no use for amateurs on the stage, but when he heard Dickens read from a play, Macready observed, "he reads as well as an experienced actor would—he is a surprising man." (MacKenzie, 73) Macready too would become a lifelong friend; Dickens' next book, *The Life and Adventures of Nicholas Nickleby*, contains a sequence in which Nicholas joins a traveling theater company, and Dickens dedicated the book to Macready.

The events of the year—including Catherine's astonishing miscarriage at three months, a few days after Mary's death—had delayed Charley's christening until December 9, 1837. It was John Dickens who called out "Boz" when the minister asked the child's name; the child was registered as Charles Culliford Boz Dickens. The wealthy philanthropist Angela Burdett Coutts agreed to be godmother; the heiress to two fortunes, she often asked Dickens' advice on which charities she should support. She said of her wealth, "What is the use of my means but to try to do some good with them?" Her first impression of Dickens was that he appeared to be a man of "frank sincerity" and a "rather overpoweringly energetic personality." (Schlicke, 127)

OLIVER TWIST, NICHOLAS NICKELBY, AND BENTLEY'S MISCELLANY

Nicholas Nickleby was to be an attack on the ill-reputed Yorkshire schools. Before beginning the book, he and Hablot Browne ("Phiz") traveled to Yorkshire on a blustery winter day. He had seen the schoolmasters' ads offering to board and educate boys for as little as £14 annually, with no vacations unless the parents so desired. An unwanted child could be shipped off to the lonely Yorkshire moors, no questions asked.

On the pretext of finding a place for a widow to send her son, Dickens and Phiz visited several schools. At Bowes Academy they met the one-eyed schoolmaster, William Shaw, who would later bring suit against Dickens for defaming him as Wardlow Squeers, the school-master of the fictive Dotheboys Hall. Shaw recalled that while he and Dickens were talking the other gentleman sketched him; Phiz drew a man with two eyes.

Dotheboys Hall, Dickens said, is a composite of all Yorkshire schools and Mr. Squeers an amalgamation of the schoolmasters he met. All were "blockheads and imposters to whom few considerate persons would have entrusted the board and lodging of a horse or a dog." (MacKenzie, 71) A Yorkshire lawyer warned them to tell the widow "to keep the lattle boy from a' sike scoondrels." (Johnson, 218) In the graveyard beside the school, Dickens and Phiz saw headstones of twenty-five boys between the ages of seven and eighteen. Shaw had been sued by parents of two boys who had gone blind for lack of medical care. The boys reported being beaten, fed maggot-ridden food, and often forced to sleep five to a bed. Shaw was fined, but he continued to run the school. His last advertisement appeared after *Nicholas Nickleby* came out.

Dickens' descriptions in the book had their effect in closing down Yorkshire schools, and he quickly realized that he had power through his writing to bring about social reforms. He also found he could combine humor and sorrow in one book. *Pickwick* had comedy and *Oliver Twist* pathos, but *Nickleby*, a tragicomedy, possessed both.

Dickens began *Nickleby* before *Oliver Twist* was finished even by half. Writing two novels at the same time was risky business; his energy and creativity might give out. A critic said, "Mr. Dickens writes too often and too fast" (MacKenzie, 69)—and compared him to a rocket that would fall like a stick. But the energetic Dickens didn't slow down. He had a large house to maintain and a family to support—furthermore he enjoyed the acclaim.

Charles' and Catherine's first daughter, named Mary, was born in March of 1838; the first installment of *Nickleby* appeared at the end of that month and sold some 50,000 copies on its first day.

For the summer holiday, the Dickenses rented a country cottage and played host to friends and family. His parents and brother came, Catherine's sister Fanny and her husband Henry Burnett, and Dickens' sister Letitia, who was now married to Henry Austin. Forster was there as well, serving as president and keeper of rubber balloons for the "Gammon Balloon Aeronautical Association," a club Dickens organized to delight the children.

By November *Oliver Twist* was out, the first of Dickens' works to be published under the author's own name. The public now could identify Boz with Dickens. Still, there were problems. One troubling and expensive annoyance was plagiarism. There were at the time no laws to keep an author's works from being dramatized without his participation or consent. Often a story would be staged before the ending was printed. One representation of *Oliver Twist* so disgusted Dickens that he lay down in his box, refusing to move until the curtain came down.

With Phiz, Dickens made another trip north, this time to see the cotton mills. He wrote to Catherine that the industrial north was a "lurid and melodramatic horror." He saw "miles of cinder paths, and blazing furnaces, and roaring steam engines," and had never seen "such a mess of dirt, gloom, and misery," (Johnson, 224) He could not "deal with those dust-laden mills and their thunderous machines." (225) The horrors of nineteenth-century industrialism that wound through factory towns like a malignant growth was more than his pen could handle. Not until fifteen years later, in the mournful *Hard Times*, would he strike a "sledgehammer blow" (a favorite expression) to the ruthless mills and the plight of the helpless workers.

Dickens' success grew by leaps and bounds with the popularity of *Nickleby*. Influential new friends introduced him into London society. The boy who had pasted labels on shoe blacking and educated himself in the British Museum was in no way intimidated by those who had come out of universities and from homes with formal gardens and galleries. Although he was dapper and somewhat dandyish in his flaming waistcoats and gold jewelry, he also made an impression with his witty and energetic conversation. The Athenaeum Club, a gathering of men of achievement, offered Dickens a membership in June of 1838, at the early age of twenty-six. He knew he had reached a pinnacle of fame by this invitation to join men of letters, scientists, and statesmen.

During this time, troubles with Bentley loomed over editorship of the *Miscellany*. After many disagreements Dickens resigned, suggesting Harrison Ainsworth as editor. One sore point between Dickens and Bentley was Bentley's insistence on delivery of the novel, *Barnaby Rudge* and that Dickens, except for finishing *Nickleby*, was to work exclusively on *Rudge*. They eventually resolved their differences by Dickens buying back the rights to *Oliver Twist*, which had run in the *Miscellany*, with the understanding that he would no longer provide Bentley with any of his writings. Dickens said Chapman and Hall—"the best book publishers, past, present, and to come" (Johnson, 52)—would be his only publishers. Winning the three-year battle with Bentley, combined with his increasing sense of his power as a writer, gave Dickens the confidence that he could triumph over anyone who got in his way.

Kate Macready Dickens, Charles' second daughter, was born on October 29, 1839. With this addition to the family, Dickens felt the time had come for them to move into a larger and more elegant home than Doughty Street afforded. He found it at No. 1 Devonshire Terrace. A friend, "a genius in houses" suggested "elaborate installation of water closets." (Johnson, 269)

MASTER HUMPHREY'S CLOCK

The unhappy experience of editing the *Miscellany* had not suppressed Dickens' desire to edit another magazine. He wrote to Forster of a new vision: of a gentle old Master Humphrey and the grandfather clock in which this man kept a stack of tales and adventures. The old man's friends would gather around his fireside to hear him read the stories.

The first publication of *Master Humphrey's Clock* appeared in April while Dickens and Catherine were in Birmingham visiting his brother Alfred, who was in training there to become an engineer. Forster met them with the news that *Master Humphrey's Clock* had sold 70,000 copies, and they quickly spent all of their money in celebration and had to pawn their watches to pay for their train fares home. But sales dropped off with the next two issues; readers had expected the start of another novel. To bide his time until he found a way to save *Clock*, Dickens had Mr. Pickwick and Sam Weller join Master Humphrey's fireside.

The novelist got the idea for a children's story while watching a "Punch and Judy" show where he saw a scruffy old man and a little girl. He visualized them in a shop of ancient odds and ends, a "curiosity shop." *The Old Curiosity Shop*, whose themes are greed and the evils of gambling, is a kind of fairy-tale melodrama of a gambling grandfather fleeing with the saintly Little Nell from the bogeyman dwarf Quilp. Among the thirty characters they meet are the owners of a Punch and Judy show, a waxworks, and a troupe of dancing dogs. Dickens wrote to Forster that he laughed out loud at the antics of Dick Swiveller and Mrs. Jarvey and her traveling waxworks. Of Little Nell, he told Macready, "I am slowly murdering that poor child.... It wrings my heart. Yet it must be." Mary Hogarth was still very much in his thoughts, and his words to Forster on Nell echoed his words on Mary: "Nobody will miss her like I shall." (MacKenzie, 98)

He finished the book in January of 1841. On the last page he had Master Humphrey return to begin the story of *Barnaby Rudge*. Dickens knew he must give his readers another serialized novel, and Chapman and Hall were expecting the same.

On February 8, 1841, Charles and Catherine welcomed another son, their fourth child, whom they called Walter Landor Dickens. (Walter Savage Landor was the child's godfather.)

Barnaby Rudge had been hanging over Dickens' head like a dark cloud ever since the grievances with Macrone and Bentley. At the center of the book's plot were the anti-Catholic Gordon Riots of 1780, but the book contained elements of the human drama Dickens' readers loved, as well: a father-son conflict, an unsolved murder, a seduction, a hanging, a half-witted hero, and a slightly mad anti-Catholic agitator. A rare bright spot was Dolly Vardon, whose little flower-trimmed hats inspired a popular song:

> Dolly, Dolly, Dolly, Dolly Vardon
> Dressed in a little flowery garden
> (Cooper, 82)

In the middle of the story, as he narrated the rioters' storming of Newgate Prison, Dickens wrote to Forster, "I think I can make a better riot than Lord George Gordon did." (MacKenzie, 98)

THE AMERICAN EXPEDITION

The prospect of traveling to America had been in Dickens' mind for some time.

Dickens had confessed to Forster that he feared he might run out of creativity and needed to take a break. He recalled that Sir Walter Scott "had ruined his best work ... *because he never left off.*" (MacKenzie, 105) Chapman and Hall agreed to give him a year's rest from writing and a monthly advance toward future works, and in September he wrote to Forster, "I HAVE MADE UP MY MIND (WITH GOD'S LEAVE)

TO GO TO AMERICA." (Johnson, 358) He planned to go soon after
Christmas; like Tony Weller in *Pickwick*, he would run over to "Merrika"
(MacKenzie, 106) and write a book upon return about "Merrikans."
Catherine was in tears with anxiety over leaving her children, but when
the Macreadys offered to take care of the children, and knowing that her
maid, Anne, would go along, she gave in. In the issue of *Master
Humphrey's Clock* in which the last chapter of *Barnaby Rudge* appeared,
Dickens announced his plans to visit America—with the promise of
another novel in short order.

Dickens and Catherine boarded the *Britannia* on January 4, 1842
for about an eighteen-day sail to Boston. Dickens described the small
ship to his artist friend David Maclise as "a gigantic hearse with windows
in the sides and a melancholy stove at one end" (MacKenzie, 109) and
the bed in the tiny stateroom as "a muffin beaten flat." (Johnson, 362)
After a rough crossing, they steamed into Boston Harbor to be greeted
by a dozen reporters rushing up the gangplank to shake hands. The
reporters couldn't mistake Charles Dickens, who had decked himself out
in a shaggy fur coat, a frock coat, a red embroidered waistcoat with a
gold watch chain, and a huge folded cravat with two diamond tiepins.

One reporter, on learning Dickens had yet not booked a hotel
room, dashed off to do so. Crowds peppered the dock, shouting, "Is
Little Nell dead?" They were eagerly—anxiously—awaiting the last
chapter of *The Old Curiosity Shop*.

Glowing with excited anticipation of all that lay ahead, Dickens
bounded into the hotel, shouting, "Here we are!" (Johnson, 365) After
dinner, he and Lord Mulgrave, a shipmate, braved the cold and under a
full moon explored Boston. Dickens raced over the sparkling snow
laughing and shouting, pointing out houses and signs in shops.

From the first day of their arrival, Dickens and Catherine were
inundated with invitations to dinners and receptions. Admirers jammed
the hotel entrance waiting to see Boz; they even pulled off pieces of his
fur coat as souvenirs. In letters home, Dickens told of crowds that lined
the streets, audiences that cheered him in his seat at the theater, and
congratulatory letters by the ton. Catherine wrote to Fanny, "The
people are most hospitable. We shall be killed by kindness."
(MacKenzie, 113)

And in turn he was impressed when he visited institutions. He saw
children's happy faces at the Institute for the Blind. Inmates at the State
Hospital for the Insane were encouraged to do useful work. Girls in the

mills at Lowell had extra comforts, such as plants and a library. He visited Harvard and made a lasting friendship with one professor there, the poet Henry Wadsworth Longfellow.

Here was a great quantity of food for the imagination. In a letter to Forster, he wrote, "I have a book already." He praised the Americans for their humanely run institutions and apparent wealth of opportunity. He wrote, "There is not a man in this town ... who has not a blazing fire and a meat dinner every day of his life." (Johnson, 371)

The highlight of the Boston visit was a $15-per-person banquet with band provided and more than forty choices of foods. Dickens stood up to give a speech, to tumultuous applause. He expressed thanks for the warm welcome and gave praise for America. He said, "he had dreamed for years of setting foot on this shore and breathing this pure air." (Johnson, 375) He concluded by speaking on the copyrights of authors; he hoped American authors, he said, would recoup some profit from England for their work and that English authors would gain profit in America. The next day, the newspapers criticized him for bringing up issues of international copyright at a social gathering, at a banquet given in his honor. They called him a "mercenary scoundrel." (Johnson, 382)

Regardless, he remained a popular figure. One said, "I never saw a face fuller of vivid action or an eye fuller of light and he is so freely animated—*so unlike our folks*." (MacKenzie 112–113) But some referred to his crude habits—such as combing his hair at the dinner table and wearing too much jewelry—and to his elaborate, somewhat vulgar velvet waistcoats (when men of Boston wore coats of plain black satin).

At a dinner in Connecticut, Dickens spoke again on the subject of copyright law, telling the audience that he intended to take every opportunity to bring up the words *international copyright*. One newspaper declared critically that his only purpose in coming to the United States was to push a copyright law through Congress. This opposition increased his determination to work for his cause.

By the time they reached New York—where Dickens seems at some point to have contracted frostbite in his left foot—the public's continued adulation had become a burden. "I can do nothing that I want to do," he said. "... If I turn into a street I am followed by a multitude. If I stay at home, the house becomes, with callers, like a fair." (Johnson, 383) Except for two already scheduled events, a ball and a dinner, he would accept no more invitations. The "Boz Ball," the climax of his visit to New York, was grand. The hall had been decorated lavishly and even excessively, replete with statues of Apollo and Cupid, American and English flags, medallions of Dickens' works, and Dickens' portrait displayed under a golden eagle.

Horace Greeley's *The New York Tribune* was one newspaper that defended Dickens. The editors stated that authors were entitled to what had been unjustly taken from them; readers were urged to petition Congress for justice to authors. Before Dickens left New York, some of the most well-established American authors gave him a petition they had signed that demanded an international copyright law, with a request that he deliver the petition to Henry Clay in Washington.

On the floors of both houses of Congress, he met several senators and congressmen. (He found Congress no better or worse than Parliament, although he observed that more swearing and bickering went on in Congress.) He was ushered in to meet President Tyler. The president welcomed him by remarking on his youthful appearance. Dickens wanted to return the compliment, but found he couldn't to a man who seemed so tired and old. They shook hands and sat more or less looking at each other until Dickens excused himself on the grounds that the president must be busy. While in Washington, he passed on the copyright petition to Henry Clay; he was pleased to learn that Clay had been trying to pass a copyright law since 1837.

Each letter sent home showed a decline in his enthusiasm for America. He had a few adjectives to describe American virtues— "warmhearted," "generous," "obliging"—but he found their bad habits disgusting. He said he could almost stand the habit of spitting if they would "spit clean," but it was a horrible mixture of saliva and tobacco juice. Although there were spittoons everywhere, even beside President Tyler's desk, they spit on the carpet all the same.

His criticisms did not end with social niceties. He called slavery "an accursed and detested system." (MacKenzie, 122) At a slave auction he saw a man's wife and children sold away from him, and being waited on by a slave gave him a sense of shame. "This is not the republic I came to see," he wrote to Forster. "This is not the republic of my imagination." (Johnson, 404) After Richmond, Virginia, the Dickenses had planned to go to South Carolina; but Dickens declared he would go no further south—not into the land of slavery.

An uncomfortable journey was ahead as they went west through sparsely settled country. A paddlewheel steamer took them down the Ohio River and up the Mississippi—"the beastliest river in the world"

(MacKenzie, 123)—to St. Louis. They went no farther west. He wanted to see the prairie; he found that "the great plain was like a sea without water, unbroken except by one thin line of trees, bare and lonely." (Johnson, 412)

Catherine carried with her the painting of the children that Maclise had given her; Dickens' traveling secretary, George Putnam, had instructions to unpack it each time they settled in. A ship arrived at one point with letters from home that gladdened her for days. Still, she was miserably homesick. Too, her constant stumbling and falling exasperated Dickens; "She falls into or out of every boat or coach we enter," he wrote to Forster. Still, she had made a "most admirable traveler," he said. "She has never given way to despondence or fatigue ... has always accommodated herself well and cheerfully to everything." (Johnson, 414)

A steamer took them back to Cincinnati. For a day and a night they traveled by stagecoach to Columbus. George Putnam had been indispensable, seeing to their lodging, their luggage, and the pile of letters from strangers. He had even given his all in trying to shield Catherine from a passenger's flying tobacco spittle during the stagecoach ride. To get them to Sandusky, Ohio, Dickens hired a private coach. For once, they were by themselves, but bumping over a corduroy road (logs laid across swampy ground), Charles had to tie a handkerchief on each side of the coach for Catherine to hang onto, so that she wouldn't wind up in "a heap on the floor" or "crush her head against the roof." After dark, the coach left the corduroy road, and they drove into a thunderstorm.

They spent the night in a room at a log tavern, where Catherine said she was "almost devoured by bugs." (Johnson, 416) From Sandusky it was on to Buffalo and Niagara Falls. Dickens was eager to see the Falls and to hear the roar of the rushing water, and it seems he was not disappointed: he wrote home of his awe of those waters, "rolling, tumbling, and leaping all day long with bright rainbows making fiery arches down a hundred feet below us." (Johnson, 418)

A sail across the river took them onto Canadian soil. Seeing an English Sentinel was for Dickens like being at home, even if the man wore his boots over his trousers and a fur cap. They met Lord Mulgrave, their shipmate from the *Britannia*, in Montreal. The earl was involved with a theatrical performance for charity. Dickens didn't have to be asked twice to be stage manager and actor. He later described his own performance as "very funny" and congratulated Catherine on playing her part "devilishly well." (Johnson, 424-25)

For the long-awaited trip home, Dickens opted for a sailing vessel rather than a steamship in the hope they might have a smoother crossing. The *George Washington* sailed on June 7 and reached Liverpool three weeks later. Dickens got up a musical group during the voyage, the "United Vagabonds," to entertain the passengers. He played his accordion; one played the violin, and another the bugle.

The children were in bed when the Dickens arrived at Devonshire Terrace, but he awoke them for embraces. He embraced the Macreadys, too, and then sought Forster.

THE FRUITS OF THE AMERICAN EXPEDITION

Settled in once again—it was at about this time that Catherine's sister Georgina, who would become Dickens' Muse, took up residence with the couple—Dickens got to work almost immediately on *American Notes*, the travel book he had promised to Chapman and Hall. To jog his memory of the trip he borrowed letters he had written to Forster and friends. The author said it was "a day to day record of things that passed under his eyes" and his reaction to them. His goal was to write "honestly and fairly" of what he had seen. (Johnson, 433)

Longfellow came for a visit to Devonshire Terrace and read the proofs. He called it "jolly and good-natured" but "at times very severe." He thought Dickens' chapter on slavery was "grand." (Johnson, 441) Overall, the reactions were not so positive; although many agreed with his aversion to spitting and slavery, and he did pay tribute to the American people, his audience understood from subtext that he had not liked the country as a whole.

An editor for *The Edinburgh Review* sent the book back with the comment, "I cannot praise it; and I will not cut it up." Dickens did not expect compliments from the American press, and he did not receive them; one newspaper scoffed that his only praise for Niagara Falls was as he saw it from the Canadian side, and another derided Dickens' view as that of a "narrow-minded, conceited cockney." (Johnson, 442)

The experience in the United States would inspire a complete reworking of Dickens' next book, whose theme was the unbridled expansion of human selfishness. He had difficulty in naming the book and the hero. Sweezlewag came to mind and Chuzzleboy, Chubblewig, Chuzzlewag. The book finally became *The Life and Adventures of Martin Chuzzlewit.*

There are two Martins in *Chuzzlewit*: the grandfather who suspects the family is after his money, and the egotistical grandson, who thinks of no one but himself. It was not his original story plan, but Dickens sent young Martin to America because of the criticism of *American Notes* and in hopes of increasing book sales. He wrote more disparagingly of the country in *Chuzzlewit* than he had in *Notes.* "Martin has them all stark, raving mad across the water," Dickens told Forster. (Johnson, 439)

The overwhelming response to *A Christmas Carol* made Christmas of 1843 truly a season of joy. That *Martin Chuzzlewit* did not achieve the financial success of his other novels did not impede the celebration.

But the new year brought with it new financial troubles. The fifth Dickens child, Francis Jeffrey, was born in January, and Charles' father John sought yet more money. When Dickens heard of his losses over *Carol*, he decided that he must go to Italy, where living was cheaper. Making arrangements to transport five children, Catherine, her sister Georgina, three women servants, his courier, himself, and a dog from London to Genoa required the purchase of a large caravan. He found and acquired a "good, old shabby, devil of a coach" that could not move without the pulling of four horses. (MacKenzie, 154)

GENOA AND THE RETURN TO JOURNALISM

The last installment of *Chuzzlewit* came out on July 1, and on July 2 the Dickens entourage set out for Paris. After two weeks of rumbling through small French towns and over waterways where they had to be hoisted onto barges, they arrived in Genoa. The carriage rolled up to a rusty, sagging gate that opened into a weedy, unkempt courtyard. The building beyond that Dickens called the "pink jail" was the Villa Bagnerello. Inside they went up a cracked marble staircase that led to dozens of rooms, occupied by bats, rats and fleas. Dickens wrote Forster of the "old, wandering, ghostly, echoing, grim bare house" that had been rented for them by a friend of a friend. (Johnson, 509) When the three months' lease had expired, they moved to the Palazzo Peschiere, which Dickens called "a palace in a fairy tale." (MacKenzie, 157)

Dickens enjoyed Italy's scented gardens and orange groves as well as swimming in the Mediterranean, but his letters to England suggested a certain homesickness. He had a Christmas book to write, for which he had an idea but no title. He had always needed a working title to get started, and the surroundings were not conducive to settling down to write. The bells of Genoa never ceased their tolling. But one day, while the bells clanged and the water in the fountains sparkled, it came to him: "The Chimes." Like *Carol*, the story made a case for charity and mercy, and like *Carol*, *The Chimes* sold well; but *Chimes* never reached *Carol*'s popularity. (Another product of this period was his travel book, *Pictures from Italy*, which he wrote from the point of view of an observant tourist. This was not published until 1846.)

Dickens befriended a Swiss banker, Emilio de la Rue, who lived in the nearby Palazzo Rosso. His wife, Augusta, suffered headaches and insomnia and had visions of a frightening phantom. Dickens, who had been interested in mesmerism for some time and had relieved Catherine's headaches with hypnosis, offered to help Augusta. After several treatments, he believed she had improved, but his spending more time with her, at odd hours, disturbed Catherine.

On June 19, he and Catherine left Genoa to travel through southern Italy. Dickens told Emilio de la Rue that he would keep in touch and asked him to report on his wife's condition. The de la Rues met them in Rome, and all traveled north together. Dickens' treatments continued to help Augusta, but he was giving her all his time, and Catherine became increasingly irritated. She no longer spoke to the de la Rues, and she complained of her husband's neglect; the situation was putting a strain on their marriage. They returned to Genoa to prepare the family and the coach for the return to London. Dickens hated to stop the treatments and promised Augusta to try telepathic hypnosis by concentrating at the same time each day.

Dickens felt a pull toward journalism again, a desire to edit his own newspaper and to use his writing power to fight social ills. Among the issues he wished to address was capital punishment. A hanging he had seen haunted his memory; he recalled vividly "the two forms dangling ... the man's, a loose, limp suit of clothes as if the man had gone out of them; the women's fine shape, so elaborately corseted and artfully dressed, that it was quite unchanged in its trim appearance as it slowly swung from side to side." (MacKenzie, 218) The sight had nauseated him, and the memory still did. He thought of using his power as a writer and as a public figure to do something about it.

On October 28, 1845, Catherine bore her sixth child, Alfred d'Orsay Tennyson Dickens. Less than one month later, on November 17, Dickens became editor of *The Daily News*. He hired a staff, putting his father, who did have some journalistic experience, in charge of reporters. The first issue ran his Christmas story for 1845, *Cricket on the Hearth: A Fairy Tale of Home*. In this tale, significantly, a man thinks his wife is being unfaithful but a cricket assures him that it is not so.

Dickens' two travel books and the last two Christmas stories had dimmed his popularity, and he needed to come up with something fresh and impressive; also, he had forgotten the long hours of work a morning newspaper required. After only two weeks, he told Forster he was resigning to go abroad for a new book, and Forster agreed to take over the newspaper.

DOMBEY AND SON, THE BIRTH OF SOCIAL ACTIVISM, AND TWO TRAGIC LOSSES

The family embarked in June of 1846, traveling first by train and then to Lausanne, Switzerland in three coaches. Dickens wrote to Forster that he was off to a good start on his new novel, *Dombey and Son*. The book was to do to pride what *Chuzzlewit* had done to selfishness; Thackeray, who had just published *Vanity Fair*, called the writing of Paul's death "stupendous." "There's no writing against such power as this," he said. "One has no chance." (Ackroyd, 521) Between writing chapters of *Dombey*, Dickens finished the Christmas story for 1846— *Battle for Life: A Love Story*, of a girl who gives up her lover for her sister. The story was criticized as impossible and absurd.

Dickens had planned to spend some time in Paris. Devonshire Terrace was rented until the summer, but with Catherine due to deliver their seventh child, they hurried back to London where Sidney Smith Dickens was born on April 18, 1847.

It is at this point that Dickens' fascination with the "fallen woman" seems to have flourished. In November of 1847, Dickens and Angela Coutts, Charley's godmother, established a home for fallen women in Shepherd's Bush, North London. Dickens leased a building, shopped for linens, and found a second-hand piano and a set of books. The home for reformed prostitutes, Urania Cottage, became a haven for other homeless women, as well; it was a place where Dickens could exercise his social conscience and feed his writer's curiosity by keeping in touch with neglected members of society. (Letters Dickens wrote to the governess who ran the Cottage, Georgina Morson, between 1849 and 1854 were discovered quite by accident and auctioned in July of 2001. They evince a very sober concern on Dickens' part for the welfare of the marginalized and detail the workings of Urania Cottage, which was unique in its day.) Dickens penned a leaflet in 1849, entitled "An Appeal to Fallen Women," in which he addressed "a woman—a very young woman still— who was born to be happy and has lived miserably; who has no prospect before her but sorrow, or behind her but a wasted youth; who, if she has ever been a mother, has felt shame instead of pride in her own unhappy child," painting the grimmest possible picture of such a course of life, and recommending the home founded by Angela Coutts as a means of redemption. The path to such redemption, curiously, lay not in social reform but in behavioral reform: "You must resolve to set a watch upon yourself," he wrote, "and to be firm in your control over yourself, and to restrain yourself; to be gentle, patient, persevering, and good tempered. Above all things, to be truthful in every word you speak. Do this, and all the rest is easy." To this affecting leaflet Dickens devoted all his skill, and its final appeal to its audience—it was distributed among prostitutes in prison—is well worth quoting as an example of fine rhetoric:

> Whether you accept or reject [the prospect of life at Urania Cottage], think of it. If you awake in the silence and solitude of the night, think of it then. If any remembrance ever comes into your mind of any time when you were innocent and very different, think of it then. If you should be softened by a moment's recollection of any tenderness or affection you have ever felt, or that has ever been shown to you, or of any kind word that has ever been spoken to you, think of it then. If ever your poor heart is moved to feel truly, what you might have been, and what you are, oh think of it then, and consider what you may yet become.

Dombey and Son was finished, and critics were exclaiming that Dickens was back and in fine form. He was looking forward to relaxing at his favorite getaway, the seaside town of Broadstairs, when he learned that his sister Fanny was gravely ill with tuberculosis and rushed to her bedside. Sitting with Fanny during her last days brought back memories of his childhood: he saw himself as a lonely boy wandering the streets of London or pasting labels on awful bottles of shoe blacking, and his father in debtors' prison. (He never spoke of those days, even to Catherine.) Fanny lingered through the summer of 1848 but died in September, her crippled son, Augustus, following shortly thereafter.

Then Dickens learned that Louis Roche, his helpful courier, who had trekked with him back and forth through Italy, France, and Switzerland, had fallen ill. Dickens took him from his lodging and with Miss Coutts' aid sent him to a hospital. The "faithful, affectionate, devoted man" (Johnson, 653) died soon afterward.

These tragedies made getting into the proper temperament for writing difficult, and amateur theatricals continued to claim a portion of his attention; but Dickens managed a story, *The Haunted Man*, for Christmas of 1848. Perhaps at the time, Dickens was contemplating his sorrows; the story is of a man who is offered memory loss to forget the pain of his life—but, when he finds that the price of this is the loss of his joys as well, asks that his memory be restored.

Another child arrived on January 15 of the following year, their eighth, named Henry Fielding Dickens. Inspired perhaps by the loss of two close members of his circle—especially by the time spent by Fanny's side—Dickens considered writing an autobiography. He sent pages of his boyhood experiences to Forster, but when he came to that time of life with Maria Beardnell, the memory of a lost love was too painful to put into words. Rather than an autobiography, he decided to weave his own history into fiction. He chose a working title: *The Copperfield Survey of the World as it Rolled.*

DAVID COPPERFIELD AND HOUSEHOLD WORDS

In the preface to *David Copperfield* Dickens writes that no one can love their children any more dearly than he loves his own. "But, like most fond parents, I have in my heart of hearts a favorite child. And his name is DAVID COPPERFIELD." The book opens with a curious assertion of self-doubt: "Whether I shall turn out to be the hero of my own life or whether that station will be held by anybody else, these pages must show."

Writing *Copperfield* was a strain on Dickens emotionally. He told Forster that at one point "I turned myself inside out. Though I know what I want to do, I am lumbering like a stage wagon." (MacKenzie, 214) He knew some of his characters. Mr. Micawber, a man like his own father; charming, humorous, irresponsible, and always "hoping for something to turn up." Mrs. Micawber is much the same as Dickens' mother, but perhaps better grounded. He patterned David's Dora after the petulant young Maria Beadnell, and Agnes after the sensible Mary and Georgina Hogarth. It is Dickens' own story, thus David has to work in the bottling factory, learn shorthand, and be a parliamentary reporter.

Dickens also came upon a fishing village near Yarmouth, a place to send young David. The locale brought back memories of Chatham dockyard and the River Medway.

To relieve the tension of writing David's unhappy childhood, he kept busy with Urania Cottage, taking the position of unpaid superintendent. And with his usual concern for others, he questioned the "fallen women" about their pasts and hopes for their future. *David Copperfield* began to appear in 1849.

The year 1850 was a memorable one for Dickens. His first-born, Charley, did admirably well at Eton, and his ninth child by Catherine, Dora Anne, arrived on August 16. With the founding of *Household Words*, a weekly magazine, Dickens turned a corner in his career. He served as editor and half-owner, dividing the other half among Forster, the printers Bradbury and Evans, and assistant editor, William Wells. Owning the magazine afforded Dickens an opportunity to air grievances against suffering and injustice without the interference he had experienced with *Bentley's Miscellany* and *Master Humphrey's Clock*.

By the year's end, the magazine was making a healthy profit for Dickens and his partners. Sales of *Copperfield*, which ran until November, were low as compared to those of his other novels, but it was praised for its "easy originality" and called "the best of all the author's fictions." (MacKenzie, 225)

The following year, 1851, did not shape up well. Dora was diagnosed with "congestion of the brain," and Catherine suffered a nervous breakdown. John Dickens died on March 31, his son Charles by his side; Dora died just two weeks later.

Owing to the family's grief, his play *Not so Bad as We Seem*, to be given as a command performance for Queen Victoria, had to be postponed; but it did finally go forth. The Duke of Devonshire lent Devonshire House for the performance and had a special box built for the Queen. The play was so well received that the Duke asked that it be repeated.

Dickens' new residence, the eighteen-room Tavistock House, boasted a drawing room large enough for thirty people. It also had a schoolroom, which he envisioned making into a theater with a stage. They leased the house, and he spent a fretful summer running back and forth from Broadstairs to fuss over the workers doing repairs and alterations; the work was completed by November. The seventh son, Edward Bulwer-Lytton Dickens, was born on March 13, 1852.

BLEAK HOUSE, HARD TIMES, AND LITTLE DORRIT

It is at this time that Dickens began work on his new novel, *Bleak House*, in which he assailed the British judicial system, which "corrupted and ruined everyone in it except the lawyers." (MacKenzie, 247) The complex and sensational plot deals with a protracted lawsuit, a suicide, a murder, an illegitimate birth, and a series of mysteries. *Bleak House* ran between 1852 and September of 1853.

Shortly after Dickens returned from touring Italy with friends (including the novelist Wilkie Collins), Dickens began the public readings from his works for which he would become even more famous. An old kidney problem flared up, too, for which Dickens' doctor advised rest; the family moved to Boulogne for the summer, where Dickens finished *Bleak House* and thirty-nine episodes of *A Child's History of England*, which he had been preparing for *Household Words*. Dickens would return to Boulogne in the second half of 1854.

In 1839, Dickens had gone north and seen the misery in the factory system. He made a return trip in 1854 to Preston to find little improvement. He despaired over the unsatisfactory treatment of factory workers, half-starved in their squalid makeshift houses. What he had seen on each visit he wrote into *Hard Times*, a book which stresses the point that children need gaiety in their lives to stimulate imagination and that they should be taught that concern for others is more important than money.

The following year, Dickens received an ill-fated letter, one with familiar handwriting: Maria Beadnell had written to suggest that they meet. He seized on the opportunity to see her again, but the meeting proved to be disappointing. She was married with two daughters, and had grown fat, as she had warned him. What had been an alluring laugh had become an annoying giggle. The Maria of his memory, his great love, was cruelly shown no longer to exist. Still, as he had used her in *Copperfield*, he could use her again; she would appear as Flora Flinching in his next novel, *Little Dorrit*.

Dorrit is very autobiographical. In it, the character Arthur, who loved Flora in his youth, returns to find her fat and silly. Dickens again ensconced his characters in the Marshalsea; William Dorrit lives there long enough to become known as "the Father of the Marshalsea." Little Amy Dorrit lives there with him. The novelist gave his vision of society as a sort of prison that catches people in a web until they can free themselves through love. (Little Dorrit finds love with Arthur and leaves the prison to marry him.)

While he was writing *Dorrit*, which ran between 1855 and June of 1857, his friend Wilkie Collins pitched a play that he wanted Dickens to produce. *The Frozen Deep* was a melodrama about two men in love with the same woman; the jilted one (to be played by Dickens) died in rescuing his love-rival, lost on an Arctic expedition. Tavistock House became a theater, complete with backstage activity and Dickens running the show.

At that time Gad's Hill Place, the house his father had said he might own someday, was put up for sale. Living there, in sight of Rochester Castle and the River Medway, would be a return to the happiest time of Dickens' life. He bought the house in 1856 and began renovations shortly thereafter.

THE END OF THE HOGARTH MARRIAGE;
PUBLIC READINGS

The Frozen Deep, which too would be performed before the Queen, went on to Manchester, with members of the theatrical Ternan family in the cast. Dickens, at this time, became infatuated with young Ellen Ternan, who was co-starring with him and her mother, and poured out his heart to Forster. He had become increasingly dissatisfied with Catherine and sensed the impending breakup of their marriage. "Poor Catherine and I," he wrote, after twenty years together and ten surviving children, "are not made for each other." (MacKenzie, 292) Angela Couts tried to dissuade the breakup, but Dickens responded that "reconciliation was unthinkable." (MacKenzie, 312) In the spring of 1858, a bracelet Dickens had bought fror Ternan was delivered to his own house—

possibly, but not certainly, in error—and Catherine accused him of conducting an affair. Dickens denied the accusation, but they separated legally in June of 1858. Rumors circulated about an affair with Georgina Hogarth; other rumors implicated an unknown actress. Within days, Dickens published annoucements defending the separation as amicable—though he and Catherine never were quite reconciled.

Dickens expected his friends to rally around him, but since the breakup many treated him coolly for what they considered his shabby behavior toward Catherine, for his assigning to her the blame for all the couple's troubles. They disapproved of his unkind assertion that she did not love her children; it is true that, with the exception of Charley, who lived with Catherine after the separation, the Dickens children saw little of their mother after that time—but by whose edict this was, is unclear, and it is certain that Catherine was not permitted to attend Kate's wedding in 1860.

An acquaintance who had not seen Dickens in a while was surprised to see deep lines and a gloomy expression on his usually smiling face.

Confused and unhappy, Dickens needed a diversion. He considered reading for profit; he had been reading *Carol* at charity functions. A means of increasing his income became necessary, too, with the expense of two houses (Tavistock and Gad's Hill) and his assistance to the Ternans.

It was at this time that he broke with Bradbury and Evans. They had shown no sympathy during his difficult domestic troubles, and he decided to divest himself of their friendship by buying out their partnership in *Household Words*. When they refused to sell, a judge put the magazine up for auction. Dickens bought it in 1859 and renamed it to *All the Year Round*; needing a story to run, he began *A Tale of Two Cities*, his second historical novel, which ran until November. With Collins' play, *The Frozen Deep*, in mind, in *Tale* he explored the plot of a man's giving his life to save his rival in love. For a better view of the French Revolution, in which the book was to be set, Dickens studied his friend Carlyle's *French Revolution*. He set out to create a tale of action that relied, for once, more on plot than on character.

A Tale of Two Cities finished, he left assistant editor Wills in charge of *All the Year Round* and toured the provinces, giving readings of the Christmas stories and *Pickwick* to enthusiastic audiences. The tour offered some consolation for his problems and, in any case, turned a handsome profit.

GREAT EXPECTATIONS, OUR MUTUAL FRIEND,
AND THE SUCCESS OF DICKENS' READINGS

Dickens had been mulling over another story of an unloved orphan boy who grows up to suffer every species of unhappiness, including that of unrequited love. When this coalesced, he again wrote in the first person, calling the product *Great Expectations*. A major character in the work was the queer Miss Havisham, jilted at the altar in the distant past and therefore frozen in time, still wearing her wedding dress, a table set with her moldering wedding cake. She teaches her ward, Estella, that a girl must break men's hearts.

Dickens now rehearsed readings from all his books. He traveled between January and June of 1862, thrilling his audiences. The pace was tiring him, but he never showed fatigue to an audience. "I'm very much used up," he told Georgina Hogarth (MacKenzie, 334), but he hated to stop, for he made far more money reading than writing.

Back at Gad's Hill for Christmas—he had taken up residence there in 1860—he wrote to Forster, confessing, "I'm trying to plan out a new book, but I have not got beyond trying." (MacKenzie, 141–142) In 1864, after several trips for readings and sojourns in Paris, Dickens finally wrote *Our Mutual Friend*, the story of two people who marry each other for money then find out that each was crushingly mistaken in estimating the other's fortune. In the macabre Dickensian fashion that recalls his early days reading illustrated penny-weeklys, in *Friend* a corpse turns up in a river and a will is sought in a dust heap. The new novel centered, again, on the theme of love conquering money, and appeared between 1864 and the fall of 1865.

Perhaps aware of Dickens' clearly failing health, an actor friend sent to him a kit of pieces to assemble into a small chalet in the Swiss style. Dickens had it placed under the trees at Gad's Hill as a peaceful place to write.

With *Our Mutual Friend* finished, Dickens was feeling the strain of his work severely and wished to escape, even briefly. He traveled to Paris with Ellen Ternan in 1865. On the return trip, while going over a bridge, his train ran off the track—and some of the cars tipped over the side into the water. Dickens climbed through a window, helped passengers out of the perilously perched car, and then passed around his flask of brandy to revive the victims. Remembering that the last copy of *Our Mutual Friend* was on the train, he crawled back into the car to save it. The wreck was a shock to both him and Ternan; it left Dickens weak for several months and nervous about riding in trains.

Dickens was keeping his two lives separate—the writer/reader, and his secret time with Ellen Ternan. His daughter Kate would later insist that her father and Ternan had a child who died; it is true that Ternan did live in seclusion for six months. Dickens paid her rent during this time under the name "Charles Tringham."

There had been several offers from America to return to give readings, with guarantees of tempting profits; Dickens sent his manager, George Dolby, to the States to find out whether there were still ripples from *American Notes* and *Martin Chuzzlewit*. Dolby returned to say the coast was clear, but Dickens still was hesitant about going. Forster did not want him to go, for Dickens' health was exacerbated by his frequent readings throughout the British Isles, and Dickens also was reluctant to leave Ternan. His left foot began to swell, an ailment he attributed to the foot's having become frostbitten in the New York snow in 1842.

Nevertheless, Dickens sailed back to Boston in November of 1867. His performances were sold out in Boston and New York. Dickens wrote to England that when Dolby once "put such an untidy heap of paper money on the table that it looks like a family wash." (MacKenzie, 362)

For the readings he carried a special stage set with a maroon curtain at the back. The desk had two shelves, for a glass and water bottle and for a handkerchief and gloves. A gasman traveled with them to adjust the lighting. Each letter from New York contained reports of bitter weather and deteriorating health. After performances in Philadelphia, Baltimore, Washington, and other eastern cities, Dickens realized he would not have the strength necessary to continue on to Chicago and Canada. Dolby worried about "the Chief's" condition. He would be hoarse and almost prostrate, but once he was on stage the voice and the energy always returned. He revived himself with "Rocky Mountain Sneezers," a purported stimulant that contained a mixture of bitters, lemon, sugar, and snow.

Dickens returned to England in 1868 a wealthier man; seventy-six readings had grossed $228,000; expenses had been about $30,000. He decided he should make a new will bequeathing £1,000 to Ternan and *All the Year Round* to Charley. Despite his health troubles, he assumed additional duties at the magazine.

And, after a few days at home, Dickens felt ready to perform again. He told Dolby to arrange bookings, planning to interpret the murder of Nancy from *Oliver Twist*. He did it for a tryout and gave such shrieking and gesticulation that, to his immense satisfaction, the listeners were "unmistakably pale and horror-stricken." (MacKenzie, 374)

The introduction of the murder to the program inspired *The Times* to comment, "He has always trembled on the boundary line that separates the reader from the actor, now he clears it by a leap." (375) But the performance of Nancy's murder took too much out of him. Dickens broke down, perhaps even suffering a stroke, and two doctors ordered complete rest. Still, four days later he was back on tour—limping on his painful foot. His doctors warned that he was in danger of paralysis. He rested for a few weeks, canceling performances scheduled for the provinces, and then begged to resume the tour; his doctors at last consented to twelve readings—no more.

THE END

Perhaps in substitution for his public readings, Dickens began a new novel. It was set in an interpretation of Rochester, of which city's famed cathedral his little writing-chalet offered a view. In 1869, Dickens gave the work a title: *The Mystery of Edwin Drood*. He planned twelve installments of *Drood* to appear in *All the Year Round*, but he would finish only six, which would run until September of 1870. Even these six imply a lack of peace; their story deals with mystery, suspicion, and the evils of opium, and a dark coldness throughout is widely felt to suggest death. The effect of Dickens' health, and of his increasing gothicism, on his thought seems clear.

More than two thousand people packed the hall for his final performance, which was in London. When he finished the last reading and the ovation died down, he addressed the audience directly, tears rolling down his cheeks: "I have enjoyed an amount of artistic delight and instruction which perhaps it is given to few men to know. From these garish lights I vanish now forevermore with a heartfelt, grateful, respectful, and affectionate farewell." (MacKenzie, 386) His face shining with his tears, he blew a kiss to the crowd and limped off to more of the applause that he had always found so nourishing.

On June 8, Dickens stayed in the chalet at Gad's Hill all day, writing; he returned to the house in the evening. Later, he said he felt unwell, and he collapsed. Death came on the evening of June 9, 1870, from a paralytic stroke.

Dickens had often expressed the desire to be buried with Mary Hogarth, or at the bottom of Rochester Cathedral; but the Dean of Westminster requested that his body lie in the Poets' Corner of Westminster Abbey, near the likes of Shakespeare and Chaucer—and so it was done. Although there would be no second half of *Drood*, Dickens, deceased at the age of fifty-eight, considered his work on earth finished: "I rest my claims to the remembrance of my country upon my published works," he said in his will, "and to the remembrance of my friends upon their experience of me." (MacKenzie, 391)

WORKS CITED

Ackroyd, Peter. *Dickens*. New York: HarperCollins, 1990.

Cooper, Lettice Ulpha. *A Hand Upon the Time: A Life of Charles Dickens*. New York: Pantheon, 1968.

Dickens, Charles. *A Christmas Carol*. New York: Garden City, 1938.

————. *David Copperfield*. New York: Dodd Mead & Co., 1984.

————. *Dombey and Son*. New York: Dodd Mead & Son, 1950.

————. *The Old Curiosity Shop*. Pleasantville, New York: Reader's Digest Association, 1988.

————. *Pickwick Papers*. London and New York: McMillan & Co., Ltd., 1899.

————. *Sketches by Boz*. Everyman's Library. New York: Dutton, 1968.

Dudgeon, Piers. *Dickens' London*. London: Headline, 1987.

Forster, John. *The Life of Charles Dickens*. New York: Charles Scribner & Son, 1905.

Guide, Fred. A Christmas Carol *and its Adaptations*. Jefferson City, North Carolina: McFarland & Co., 2000.

Johnson, Edgar. *Charles Dickens: His Tragedy and Triumph*. New York: Simon & Schuster, 1952.

MacKenzie, Norman, Jeanne MacKenzie. *Dickens: A Life*. New York: Oxford University Press, 1979.

Schlicke, Paul, ed. *The Oxford Reader's Companion to Dickens*. New York: Oxford University Press, 1999.

Schwarzbach, F.S. *Dickens and the City*. London: University of London, Athlone Press, 1979.

MEI CHIN

On the Works of Charles Dickens

It is embarrassing these days to admit to a love of Charles Dickens, and it is worse still to admit that he has moved us. For his work offends the modern taste for subtlety—for intriguing, opaque characters, elliptical conversations, and a sophisticated style of prose; his characters speak their meanings, and even their deceptions are transparent. Motivations are crystal-clear, emotions loud and messy. Henry James writes, "If we might hazard a definition of his literary character, we should, accordingly, call him the greatest of superficial novelists ... It were, in our opinion, an offence against humanity to place Mr. Dickens among the greatest novelists. For ... he has created nothing but figure."[1] To enjoy Dickens, then, is to betray the aesthetic of complexity that writers like James have made the standard.

Character is not Dickens' strength, then, but nor is plot. His storylines are not original. In *Bleak House*, a girl seeks her parentage; in *Great Expectations*, *Nicholas Nickleby*, and countless others, a boy seeks his fortune. Nor, with the understandable exception of *Edwin Drood*, are Dickens' plots particularly suspenseful, for more often than not the solutions to his mysteries are obvious. Early in *Bleak House*, for example, we know that Esther is Lady Dedlock's daughter; we surmise in *Great Expectations* that Magwich is Pip's benefactor. We know who will marry; we know who will live and who will die.

Nor can Dickens' books be praised for coherence. In form, the typical Dickensian novel is swollen in the middle with delightful and horrific adventures, episodes often connected by the weakest of filaments. The endings—in which villains are unmasked, secrets revealed, and hero and heroine married—are almost always disappointing. Certainly, the serial format of many of Dickens' works is not fertile ground for a tightly plotted storyline. (On *Nicholas Nickleby*, John Forster comments, "The plot seems to have grown as the book appeared by numbers, instead of having been mapped out beforehand."[2]) And Dickens was a fast writer—too fast for some. He wrote for a deadline—effusively, breathlessly, voluminously. "We do not like this novel-writing by scraps against time," wrote one contemporary reviewer. "With this we bid not good *speed*, but good moderation of *pace*."[3] Still, we are not expected to read Dickens with care. We skim long chunks; we linger on some passages, rereading bits of dialogue and description, and skip others. In short, we read his work largely as he produced it.

Dickens may not be sophisticated for technique, then; but many consider his particular genius to have been comedy, evident as early as *The Pickwick Papers*. The late books are not at all comical. (His friend Wilkie Collins criticized *Edwin Drood* as "the melancholy product of a worn-out brain."[4]) Nonetheless, much can be said on Dickens' comedy simply by evoking the image of Mr. Micawber embracing the weeping Mrs. Micawber—"with his waistcoat full of the heads and tails of shrimps, of which he had been partaking." What is brilliant in Dickens' early books is their rampant air of the carnivalesque, as normally neglected personalities—the mentally feeble, prostitutes, workhouse children, tax collectors—take on divine roles.

Moreover, Dickens is universal; he creates on a grand scale. "In everybody," G.K. Chesterton writes, "there is a thing that loves babies, that fears death, that likes sunlight; that thing enjoys Dickens."[5] In his work can be found food for both dandy and derelict, and all react to the same things, laughing with every jester and weeping by every deathbed. His is a world of sound, sight, smell—the clang of a punch ladle, the stink of Smithfield, the looming black dome of Saint Paul's. His personalities do not *speak*, but *thunder*; Micawber and Uriah Heep and Fagin are giants, and Dickens crams his work with such an excess of them that every page vibrates. We do not find subtlety in Dickens; rather, we find subtlety *superfluous* in Dickens. And Dickens' grandeur is suffused with an unrivaled generosity to his characters and an endearing compassion for the human condition. Chesterton describes him as an optimist and a poet of the fog—who sees the dreams within the grimy human haze. Surely, it is harder to be an enthusiastic writer than a cynical one, especially if one is, as Dickens was, acutely aware of the blights of industrial England.

DICKENS AND CHARACTER

Dickens' characters are too alive to be real. They dance. To create *one* would be an achievement, and the charm in Dickens is that he created many. He also named them magnificently—Helena Landless, Uncle Pumblechook. With just their names, these characters are already, as Virginia Woolf said, "branded upon our eyeballs." Even the most minor characters are unforgettable. No one who has read *Nickleby* can forget the hardships of Smike, but equally unforgettable is the old lunatic who makes only a brief appearance—throwing marrows and wooing Mrs. Nickleby by climbing down the chimney. For Dickens loved his creations. "I am a fond parent," he writes in the preface to *David Copperfield*, "of every child of my fancy, and ... no one can love that family as dearly as I love them." His indulgence of his "children" includes characteristic modes of dress, idiosyncrasies of speech, and table manners for each. Mr. Micawber, for example, carries a "quizzing glass" and speaks "with a certain condescending roll in his voice and a certain indescribable air of doing something genteel." Middle-aged, overweight Flora Fliching of *Little Dorrit*, who is perhaps overly fond of sherry, runs her sentences together without a stop in a manner that more than one critic has compared to that which would later make the reputation of James Joyce:

> Fliching oh yes isn't it a dreadful name, but as Mr. F said when he proposed to me which he did seven times and handsomely consented I must say to be what he used to call on liking twelve months after all, he wasn't answerable for it and couldn't help it could he, Excellent man, not at all like you but excellent man!

In some cases, his characters even have their own climates. Uriah Heep's hands are cold and wet, "as ghostly to the touch as to the sight," and after shaking one young Copperfield tries desperately to rub off the wetness. Heep demonstrates Dickens' love for even the villainous. In fact, one can argue that he often prefers his crooked characters to his virtuous ones. Certainly *we* do. We like Heep better than the angelically dull Agnes, and in the end Heep is allowed an honest exit. "Copperfield," he says, "I have always hated you. You've always been an upstart, and you've always been against me."

Nicholas Nickleby is packed with bravura personalities. There is Mr. Mantalini, who woos his wife with such gorgeous prose as "Why will it vex itself and twist its little face in bewitching nutcrackers?" There is a gin-drinking infant phenomenon. There is Mrs. Nickleby, whose stream of consciousness prattle makes her a precursor to *Little Dorrit*'s Flora Finching:

> I recollect when your poor papa and I came to town after we were married, that a young lady brought me home a chip cottage bonnet, in white and green trimming, and green Persian lining, in her own carriage, which drove up to the door full gallop;—at least, I am not quite certain whether it was her own carriage or a hackney chariot, but I remember very well that the horse dropped dead as he was turning round, and that your poor papa said he hadn't had any corn for a fortnight.

It is a tremendous frolic, often vulgar, in which Mrs. Nickleby and Mr. Mantalini are crammed beside a theatre troupe, the yellow-faced miniature-painter Miss La Creevy, the boozy ex-gentleman Newman Noggs, and a dozen others, to an ear- and eye-popping result. There is no merrier villain in it all than Squeers, schoolmaster of Dotheboys Hall, with his one eye, his one-eyed daughter, and his singular theory of pedagogy:

> C-l-e-a-n, clean, verb active, to make bright, to scour. W-i-n, win, d-e-r, der, winder, a casement. When the boy knows this out of book, he goes and does it.

Dickens' earliest villains are his most exuberant. *Oliver Twist*, written at the same time as *Nicholas Nickleby*, is in many ways *Nickleby*'s opposite. There is hell in every fireplace and corpses twitching from the gallows—and Dickens describes it with relish. In *Twist*, the streets are black, rats crawl, children die, but the bloodthirstiness is blithe. The evil in *Twist* is as inspired as the comedy in *Nickleby*, and indeed *Twist* belongs to its villains: Mr. Bumble, with his confident courting style, his brass buttons, and his big appetites; the greedy, abusive Noah Claypole; Bob Fagin, toasting sausages over the fire, his face "obscured by matted red hair" or, later, gliding through London "like a loathsome reptile." Much of *Twist* is told from its villains' point of view. We are hunted with Bill Sikes by the specter of Nancy's "widely staring eyes, so lusterless and so glassy." We are shaken out of any self-righteousness by trembling with Fagin in his cell as he waits to be hanged.

The good characters in *Twist* offer no competition; they are uninteresting. Oliver Twist himself is a boy only vaguely defined. He floats through the book waiting to be, alternately, abused, treated well, and outshone by everyone—with the exception of his equally uninteresting benefactor, Mr. Brownlow. It is curious that Dickens, who felt so much for the suffering of children, should have created so many unchildlike characters. The Artful Dodger, or Jack Dawkins, we love. But Artful is a little strutting imp, "altogether, as roistering and swaggering a young gentleman as ever stood four feet six or less, in his blutchers." Similarly we love his blundering pal Charley Bates, a romantic who is always speaking at the wrong time, hopelessly smitten with one of the prostitutes, and whose traces we find in Dick Swiveller and in Toots. For these boys are merely pint-sized Dickensian adults.

Some of the children are less lovable, indeed terrifying, such as the wild-eyed boy in *Twist* who hints darkly that he "might some night eat the boy who slept next to him." Even more menacing are the boys of Dotheboys Hall:

> Pale and haggard faces, lank and bony figures, children with the countenances of old men.... There were little faces which should have been handsome, darkened with the scowl of sullen dogged suffering, there was childhood with the light of its eye quenched, its beauty gone, and its helplessness alone remaining; there were vicious faced boys brooding, with leaden eyes, like malefactors in a jail.... [W]ith every revengeful passion that can fester in swollen hearts, eating its evil way to the core in silence, what an incipient Hell was breeding there!

It is useful to point out here that no Dickens child-hero has ever been "vicious faced." It seems that Dickens wants to paint a bleak vision of neglected children and yet, at the same time, is suggesting that the truly worthy children are never tainted in the same way, that there is a *difference* between the hero and his peers. Oliver manages to win the heart of kind Mr. Brownlow with his genteel countenance—but an Oliver more like the other workhouse boys, or those of Dotheboys Hall, would not have found Mr. Brownlow so generously inclined.

THE SAINTLY, SUFFERING CHILDREN

Affecting, and alternately frightening, as the neglected children may be, they are not nearly so awful as the children written to tweak our sympathy—Dickens' saintly children. In *Twist*, there is only one appearance by little Dick, and that one is quite enough: "I dream so much of heaven," he cries, "and Angels, and kind faces that I never see!" One can almost see the wings sprouting as he speaks. Dick is a precursor of a long row of saintly, suffering children, including young Agnes and young Florence Dombey. Little Nell, of *The Old Curiosity Shop*, is perhaps the best example. The merry and the bleak combine in *Curiosity*, with mad results. The book is commanded by the poetic, perpetually quoting, infinitely corruptible, and yet beautifully innocent Dick Swiveller and the somersaulting dwarf Quilp. Quilp is as merry a villain as Squeers, "fantastic and monkey like," dancing, hopping, and happily smacking his lips after her thirteen-year-old figure. He speaks with lusty poetry: "What a nice kiss that was—just upon the rosy part." Still, the book's central story is the tragedy of little Nell, whose name, by evoking the knell of the mourning bell, already hints at her fate, who has been called a "wash of white" by Mrs. Margaret Oliphant and a "two headed monster" by A.C. Swinburne.[6] Dickens dearly loved this particular creation. When the book was written, Dickens' sister-in-law, the cherished Mary Hogarth, had just passed away at the age of seventeen—Nell's age at the time of her death. Indeed, the critic may say that Little Nell is an example of Dickens' loving too much.

What makes the saintly Little Nell so unbearable? She renounces everything, ultimately life itself, to be loyal to her mad grandfather. She is "slender," her eyes more often than not filled with tears. She is upstaged by Quilp, by Dick, even by the other children—both the card-playing Marchioness and Kit, who delightfully marches up to the oyster shop "as bold as if he lived there" and orders the waiter to "look sharp." We cannot resist pointing out that the Marchioness and Kit actually take action against their miserable conditions and save not only themselves, but also those they love. While Nell's suffering is supposed to inspire our tears, her inaction grates on modern conceptions of womanhood. In short, she is either pretty but useless—or pretty *and* useless.

In fact, the only thing Nell accomplishes in the story is martyrdom, and there is nothing charming about the child martyr, who lacks the self-absorption that makes the child delightful. The Marchioness is more woman than child, but she is cheerful, madly funny; she enjoys cards and living itself—and ultimately saves Dick Swiveller's life. Nell, on the other hand, is a *serious* child, with the soul of an *old* woman, and her success as a sentimental creation is doubtful. Nell has often been compared to Paul Dombey in *Dombey and Son*, for both are doomed to die young; but Paul is a true child, with his combination of "melancholy and slyness"—playful, over-emotional, indulgent. He loves his sister; he loves his dog; he dislikes hard work and the cold; and it is doubtful whether he would take to the idea of self-sacrifice. His comparison to Nell is flawed, though, as little Paul is adorable for the very reasons why Nell is not.

NICHOLAS NICKELBY

As a member of the heroic class of Dickensian children, Nicholas Nickelby is more impressive than either Nell or Oliver. Though many critics have maligned him as shallow and lacking personality, he is in fact vigorous and refreshing. He is Dickens' most masculine hero. He is gallant, careless, and violent tempered—he beats Squeers and enjoys flirting with actresses and millers' daughters. He is blessed with a romantic sense of entitlement to life, so that even when penniless he will turn his nose up at employment because he feels that a salary is shabby. The accusation that Nicholas is unrealistic because he is not introspective is an unjust one. The world contains a wealth of young men like Nicholas, just as little inclined toward introspection.

But Nicholas doesn't inspire sadness, not even when his best friend dies and his uncle hangs himself out of remorse, and this is a strength. In order for a Dickens novel to be moving, as the later novels are, it must center on a convincingly tender-hearted main character, because it is through the main character that the reader ultimately experiences feelings. And Nicholas is not tearful. Oliver is pallid; we can't even feel traumatized for him when Fagin, the doomed man, screeches his name in the prison cell. Most Victorians wept for Nell, but those who now read *The Old Curiosity Shop* read it for its peripheral characters and frenetic subplots. (One of Dickens' contemporaries who was not moved by the sadness was Thackeray, who claimed to have "never read the Nelly part of the *Old Curiosity Shop* more than once, whereas I have Dick Swiveller and the Marchioness by heart.") Many see this lack of effective melodrama as narrative weakness; but it makes the work—especially *The Old Curiosity Shop* and *Nicholas Nickleby*—strangely pure. Such magnificent energy cannot really sustain sentiment, and *Nickleby* and *Curiosity* achieve a dazzle that the later, more heartbreaking novels never reach.

DAVID COPPERFIELD

David Copperfield is less outrageous, but it certainly makes us cry, for it is the book that was closest to Dickens' life and thus to his heart. While Nicholas is the earlier and more heroic hero, David *is* Dickens, or Dickens as he dreamed himself. The novel is one of Dickens tightest books, better plotted because Dickens used his own life as a blueprint. David is one of Dickens' most fascinating protagonists. The young David is deeply believable, again because he is based on Dickens' memories of childhood. He is a sensitive and nervous boy who is prone to fits and tears, and like Dickens he grows to a sensitive, nervous adulthood. In nature, David is youngest of Dickens' heroes, for, even as an adult, he is always "painfully conscious" of his youth. He is taken advantage of by waiters and bullied by landladies. Steerforth calls him "little Copperfield." Indeed, what attracts readers to David is this very childlike frailty and freshness. Betsey Trotwood sums him admirably upon hearing him announce his engagement: "Poor little couple! And so you think you were formed for one another and are to go through a party-supper-table kind of life, like two pretty pieces of confectionary, do you, Trot?" As he demonstrates in his marriage to Dora, David is incapable of providing for himself or anyone else. He is babied—by Steerforth, by Agnes, and even by Dora herself, the perpetual baby.

Steerforth takes care of him at his first school, and Betsey Trotwood and Agnes then assume the duties for the rest of his life. Like a baby, David attracts nicknames. Betsey Trotwood wraps him in shawls and christens him Trotwood, which she then shortens to Trot; Steerforth calls him by the girlish name of Daisy; Dora gives him the lisping moniker of Doady.

David is both the hero and *not* the hero. Or in his own words, "Whether I shall turn out the hero of my own life, or whether that station will be held by any body else, these pages will show." Other characters exhibit more heroic tendencies—Betsey Trotwood, Mr. Peggotty, Peggotty herself, and Mr. Micawber, who exhibits a magnificently heroic self-delusion. Steerforth, though he turns out badly, looks like the hero—radiant, Apollo-like, masculine, impeccably mannered; and these qualities become more pronounced when he is with David. David's weak, conflicted persona will set the standard for Dickens' later characters—Arthur Clenham and, ultimately, Pip. It is because of David's flaws, however, that *David Copperfield* is so highly successful a sentimental achievement. David may not be perfect, but he is always empathetic. He is not distant, as many heroes are; intellectually and emotionally, he inhabits a very familiar plane. He is more timid than Nicholas and less stirringly attractive. He has a capacity for mistakes and an innocent outlook. When David's heart breaks, the reader's heart breaks with him, and experiencing the world through his sensibilities is moving indeed.

DICKENS' WOMEN

Another striking thing about David Copperfield is the number of *women* in his life. Miss Murdstone bullies him in his early life, and then Betsey and Agnes take charge. Dickens' women have come under frequent attack for their weak personalities. Kate Dickens proclaimed it herself, famously: "My father did not understand women."[7] Clare Tomalin says that they have the sexual appeal of "wax fruit."[8] We have already discussed helpless little Nell. Kate Nickleby, in her mourning dress, is a non-character. As a prostitute Nancy in *David Copperfield*, should have *some* sexiness, but she is a little too eloquent, a little too much a mouthpiece for the misery of her profession to be anything more than a symbol. But in no one person is this "wax fruit" quality more evident than in the patient figure of Agnes. As a girl, Agnes is as irritating as

Nell; she has a complacent air of goodness and cleanliness and not a scrap of girlish whimsy. Besides, she is not as pretty as "rosy" Nell. Even at a tender age she is a little old woman, her father's "little housekeeper." We much prefer the eternally boyish David, for Agnes has a lot of virtue and no charm. Too, there is something smug about her, especially when she chastises David for his friendship with Steerforth. "I caution you that you have made a dangerous friend," she says, having been in Steerforth's company for only a matter of minutes. Relationships with Agnes are emasculating; David recalls, "I had always felt my weakness, in comparison with her constancy and fortitude, and now I felt it more and more." She is always moral, always righteous, always patient, and if there was someone after whom she was modeled—it has been suggested that she was modeled after Dickens' wife, Catherine—then that person would have been a trying acquaintance indeed.

But it is unfair to assume, as many do, that all of Dickens' heroines are heirs to either Nell or the virginal Agnes. Agnes has been compared to *Bleak House's* Esther Summerson, who is more complicated and understated. Lizzie Hexham of *Our Mutual Friend* has more problems than either Agnes or Nell; we meet her fishing corpses out of the Thames with her father, who will later be murdered. Physically, *Little Dorrit's* patient Amy Dorrit has more in common with Dickens' freaks— she is, after all, a 22-year-old with the face and figure of a girl of eleven. Emotionally—with her long night walks, her prison home, and her ambitious, musical sister named Fanny—she can be said to resemble the young Charles Dickens. The shame that weighs Amy Dorrit down is Dickens' own shame, and one that we experience acutely, for it comes fresh from Dickens' heart.

Furthermore, the deferential Agnes is foiled, or balanced, by other such characters in Dickens: Rosa Dartle, Betsey Trotwood, Mrs. Crupp, and Mrs. Micawber (to name a few). There is a Miss La Creevey for every Kate Nickleby, a Marchioness for every little Nell, and an Edith and a Susan Nipper for every Florence. Eccentric Betsey Trotwood, with her loathing of men and donkeys, is one of the world's more lovable feminists. She too has suffered greatly, though the book does not describe the specifics. Mrs. Crupp, whose appearance is but brief, is nevertheless stellar among tyrannical landladies. Of her previous tenant, she says, sensibly, "Well ma'am, he died of drink ... and smoke"—which is why, in her opinion, young gentlemen should never fall in love with barmaids. The beautifully calibrated Mrs. Micawber, despite her comic accessories, is truly moving. She is, simply put, one of the most romantic women of all time. Agnes' patience is nothing in comparison to hers. She has suffered with Mr. Micawber, and yet she refuses to see anything but the good. She loves him, fiercely, and unlike Agnes she recognizes Mr. Micawber's faults but is never scolding. "Mr. Micawber," she tells David with great gravity, "is a man of great talent." He has squandered her money and forced her to pawn her pearls, her coral, and her porcelain, and yet, as she frequently repeats, she "will—never—desert—Mr. Micawber!"

Esther of *Bleak House* is perhaps the subtlest of Dickens' heroines. Her personality owes much to David Copperfield's, and she alone can match David's insight. But she is not simply David in a bonnet. She establishes herself both as David's similar and David's opposite; with all her protests that she is not the hero of her story, we understand that she is more the hero than David—and that her self-effacing manner is a means of manipulating, delicately and tactfully, both her readers and the people around her. "I don't know how it is, I always seem to be writing about myself," she writes. "... I hope any one who may read what I write, will understand that if these pages contain a great deal about me, I can only suppose it must be because I have really something to do with them, and can't be kept out."

In many ways, Esther combines the sensibilities of David with the maternal instincts of Agnes. Like David, she is parentless, but unlike David she is self-sufficient. Like Agnes, she is a "little housekeeper." She is the one Dickensian character whose nicknames rival David's; but whereas his are babyish, hers are hypermature: Durden, Mother Hubbard, Old Woman, Dame Trot to David's Trotwood. Like David, she is endowed with Dickens' witty, compassionate insight, the sane and sensitive absorber of the mad world. Still, the voice that she offers us is artful, not brash like David's; she likes to keep mysteries from us and then confess. She is coy. She informs us, for example, of her love for Allan Woodcourt through what seems to be an offhand self-correction: "I forgot to mention—or at least I have not mentioned, that Mr. Woodcourt was the same dark young surgeon whom we had met at Mr. Badger's. Or, that Mr. Jarndyce invited him to dinner that day. Or, that he came." Esther as a narrator is excessively feminine; she has none of David's directness. She is parenthetical, verbally elusive, and yet transparent. In short, she knows how to tell a story, and how to be demure.

With the reader, Esther flirts. Not in Dora's way, giggling—but subtly, her eyes touchingly downcast, and her deliberate coyness is probably what makes some readers despise her. Esther is also beautiful, and despite her protests to the contrary she is perfectly aware of the fact. Unlike most of Dickens' virginal heroines, she is aware of the admiration she causes. Tomalin acidly remarks that Dickensian heroines are sexless enough to think their every suitor wants another sister. Not Esther. She fields her first marriage proposal soon after *Bleak House* begins, and indeed she is the character who is proposed to the most. She is as aware of Allan Woodcourt's *at*tentions as of his *in*tentions. And when her beauty is taken away by smallpox, she is grieved.

Though she is meek in her diction, she is not uncritical. "We rather thought ..." Esther ventures, on the subject of Mrs. Jellyby, "that perhaps she was a little unmindful of her home." She is honest without being offensive, and the rest of the characters depend upon her as ambassador—for Caddy, for Richard and Ada. Indeed, she arranges their engagement for them, just as she arranges the marriage between Caddy and Prince. Later, she has the grimmer task of playing ambassador between the estranged Richard and Mr. Jarndyce. It can be said that without Esther, Richard and Ada would never have married, for neither of them would have been clever enough to find the words to make it happen. This seems to be a general trend in the characters of *Bleak House*; none of them can express herself frankly. Mr. Jarndyce can say he is unhappy only by remarking on an East Wind. Only with Esther can they be honest, and more often than not she anticipates them: "Is the wind in the East to-day?" she asks Mr. Jarndyce, and he is forced to answer yes or no.

So Esther functions as a mouthpiece, and the other characters have been wise to entrust her with that task. For as a judge of personality, Esther Summerson is unparalleled. She is boundlessly generous, too, but there is acid in her sweetness, so muted that it is barely detectable. She is gently cynical toward the Jellyby family, with Mrs. Jellyby finding new African charities while the baby screams and the mutton is served raw. She is equally astute with Mr. Turveytop, who struts in the glories of his deportment. Esther is keener than David; moreover, she is aware of her own desires, and how they reflect on the people she knows. About Mrs. Woodcourt she remarks, "At one time I thought she was a story teller, and at another that she was the pink of truth. Now, I suspected that she was very cunning; the next moment, I believed her honest Welsh heart innocent and simple." There is, however, no better example of Esther's skilled assessments than her depiction of Harold Skimpole. Deliciously sly, she teaches us to dislike him without ever criticizing him—indeed, while protesting her affection. "There was honey on the table, and it led him into a discourse about Bees. He had no objection to honey, he said (and I should think not, for he seemed to like it), but he protested against the overweening assumption of Bees." It is an elegantly observed comment, and damning.

Dickens had a talent for the portrayal of arrogant, damaged women. Before *David Copperfield*, he created Edith Dombey, whose rage ultimately propels *Dombey and Son*. Rosa Dartle of *Copperfield*, with her disfigured lip and violent outbursts, is chilling and genuinely tragic. Physically, she is mesmerizing; even David cannot stop watching her or her portrait. She exerts both repulsion and allure. Her conversation is all insinuation—that is, when she is behaving. Observing Steerforth calling David "Daisy," she comments, "... [I]s it a nickname? And why does he give it to you? Is it—eh?—because he thinks you young and innocent? I am so stupid in these things." David, rather appropriately, colors in reply. "She is," Steerforth comments, "all edge"—and the violent simmer underneath Rosa's shell is apparent even when she is being polite. Of course, when the politeness is stripped away, Rosa does not simmer, but boils over: "I would have her whipped ... I would have her branded on the face, drest in rags, and cast out in the streets to starve." She of course tracks down Little Em'ly and, in a magnificent display of anger, follows through on her promise, thus cementing her reputation as the least self-contained of Dickens' female characters. Rosa has a partner in Mrs. Steerforth, a monstrous depiction of maternal love in which there are glimpses of something tender. Such lapses are not surprising in either Mrs. Steerforth *or* in Rosa, just as it is not surprising in *Dombey and Son* for Edith Dombey to foster such a passion for her little stepdaughter, Florence. Such women are embodiments of emotional extremes, loosely knit together, and set off, not hidden, by a mask of prosperity; all of Dickens' terrifying women are well-off. "You have no mother?" Mrs. Steerforth says to David. "It is a pity.... She would have been proud of you." Such women are not realistic, as is the case with most Dickensian characters, but they are compelling because the emotions of which they are dilutions are hauntingly true. Agnes is off-putting because she is too patient to be emotional; in Rosa, Mrs. Steerforth, and even Mrs. Micawber, Dickens demonstrates that he does indeed understand the degrees, and also the paradoxes, of feminine feeling.

Dora too, also of *Copperfield*, embodies a woman's contradictions, albeit in a cuter package. So often dismissed, Dora is in fact a very humane portrait of flightiness; she has insecurity, earnestness, and a passionate heart. She quarrels with David and sends back his ring; she meets his entreaties with trembling and tears. Her terror of Agnes—her fear that Agnes is "too clever"—is something with which we sympathize. She is sexy, too—practically the only heroine that Dickens allows to flirt, lisping, glancing, and tossing her ringlets. "Do you mean a compliment," she asks David, when he remarks that the weather was darker a minute before, "or has the weather really changed?" Indeed, she is genuinely bewitching, and David's infatuation with her is more lyrical than the feelings he later cherishes for Agnes. "The sun shone Dora, and the birds sung Dora. The south wind blew Dora, and the wild flowers in the hedges were all Doras, to a bud." Indeed, Chesterton goes so far as to imply that Dora's last words to Agnes, her bequeathal of David, are a betrayal. Dora, on her deathbed, becomes rational, calm, generous, and Agnes-like; and it is that, not her *physical* death, that evokes such grief.

The character of Dora is said to be modeled on Dickens' first love, the inconstant and yet alluring Maria Beadnell. We can see the prudence in David's ultimate attachment to Agnes, for it is the natural extension of his orphan feelings toward her as mother and sister. No bloom appears in his love for Agnes, no fierceness, no joy, when it is compared to the lyrically rambling first love that Dora inspires. At least the lucky David, unlike Dickens, has the advantage of being married to both. Certainly, Agnes is the sensible choice, as was Catherine Hogarth, when she is compared to Maria; but she inspires no quickening of the pulse, in David or his readers, and their union is one of contentment, not happiness.

DICKENS, ROMANCE, AND "THE HAPPY COUPLE"

Dickens, who was never lucky in love, was no more talented at describing romance. Most of his "happy" matches are not convincing; they seem "tacked on," and the brief final chapters about beaming children and cheerful households are distressingly vague. In *Bleak House*, it is hard to accept the notion of a smallpox-ravaged Esther as living happily ever after with Allan Woodcourt, but we are made to accept it nonetheless. Nicholas Nickleby, at least, marries the girl with whom he fell in love with at first sight, as befits his exuberant temperament; but most of Dickens' unions are well-advised, and for this reason they are disappointing. David chooses Agnes because ideal unions are pleasant, not passionate; and yet we are expected to believe that their marriage is both. Given the similarities between David's Agnes and Dickens' Catherine Hogarth (plain, intelligent, competent, quiet), it must be surmised that Dickens and Catherine were not happy, and while Dickens asserts that the fictional union of David and Agnes is blissful he cannot paint its bliss persuasively. Dickens, who is able to make the fantastic plausible, seems unable to render garden-variety love.

Happy marriages at the end of the story are not helped by the fact that the marriages that already exist are generally grim. This includes those of Mr. Murdstone and David's mother, Edith and Mr. Dombey in *Dombey and Son*, and, most compellingly, Matthew of *Great Expectations*—tugging his gray hair out by the roots—and the foolish Mrs. Pocket, who cares nothing about her children. As Herbert Pocket, normally a playful person, freezingly comments, "I am afraid that it is scarcely necessary for my father's son to remark that my father's establishment is not particularly brilliant in its housekeeping ... I suppose there was a time once when my father had not given matters up; but if ever there was, the time is gone." Indeed, the only really happy relationship is that of Mr. and Mrs. Micawber.

Dickens recognized in himself an attraction to the prattling and pretty; his books are filled with men who make that same mistake. Matthew Pocket and his Missus are what might have happened to Davy and Dora if Dora had lived. Meanwhile, since David is smart enough to be disillusioned quickly by Dora, the only convincing examples of fervent *young* love exist among the dimwitted and ultimately doomed— sweet, stupid Ada clinging to her deluded young Richard in *Bleak House*. Moreover, the only true romantics are the lunatics. There are the Micawbers; the marrow-throwing madman in *Nicholas Nickleby*; the epitaph-composing John Chivery, wooer of Amy Dorrit; and Toots, whose unrequited passion for Florence Dombey is among the most overflowing examples of courtship to be found in the canon. Toots attends her marriage with the courage of a gallant facing the firing squad. "The banns which consign her to Lieutenant Walters, and me to—to Gloom, you know ... may be dreadful, *will* be dreadful; but I feel that I should wish to hear them spoken. I feel that I should wish to know that the ground was certainly cut from under me, and that I hadn't a hope to cherish, or a—or a leg, in short, to—to go upon."

In 1855, an older and sadder Dickens was reunited briefly with his youth's love, the formerly "prattling and pretty" Maria Beadnell. Apparently, Maria, whom Dickens had immortalized as Dora, had in their twenty years apart become as toothless and fat as she had warned in her letters. Dickens impression of the revised object of his earlier infatuation emerges in *Little Dorrit*'s Flora Finching:

> Flora, always tall, had grown to be very broad, too, and short of breath, but that was not much. Flora, whom he had left a lily, had become a peony; but that was not much. Flora, who had seemed enchanting in all she said and thought, was diffuse and silly. That was much. Flora, who had been spoiled and artless long ago, was determined to be spoiled and artless now. That was a fatal blow.

The other half of the couple, Flora's disillusioned lover and one of Dickens' literary counterparts, is Arthur Clenham. Clenham is the first middle-aged Dickensian hero, old both in body and feeling. In *Little Dorrit*, love is stripped of its pretenses, and it dies with Flora. For Clenham, there is no "happily ever after," and Dickens makes this clear. There is no passion in his eventual union with Amy Dorrit. He enfolds Amy in his arms "as if she had been a daughter" because it is the sensible thing to do.

Amy is a caretaker of the type that we have seen manifested in Agnes and Esther. Amy's sadness, however, is that of the caretaker whose caretaking responsibilities have ended. Just as Mr. Dorrit was happier dreaming in his prison, so Amy is happier taking care of a wretched, imprisoned father. Only when Amy loses her wealth and finds herself back in her old prison cell, nursing a penniless Arthur, can she be happy. The novel's end is quiet, impoverished and resigned. Arthur and Amy marry "into a modest life of usefulness and happiness." There is no glamour, no romance, and their union will always be "in sunshine and in shade." Amy has in Arthur a father, and thus a permanent responsibility. Arthur is not smitten with Amy, but she makes him feel needed. Dickens, who has always followed the romantic conventions, now refuses to acknowledge that the conventional romantic ending is undiluted joy. There is nothing transcendent in Arthur and Amy's marriage, but it will succeed. Their contentment is more secure than the bliss of earlier books, because it purports not to realize dreams, but to fulfill more functional needs. *Little Dorrit* is a disillusioning book, and it moves the reader to tears. By no means a joyful work, it is nevertheless a success as a sentimental one.

If romance is at all expressed in Dickens, then it is through the bonds of friendship and family. The real betrayal in *Great Expectations* will be when Pip leaves Joe, and the real unrequited love not that of Pip for Estella, but that of Magwich for Pip. In *David Copperfield*, the most shattering heartbreak is between David and Steerforth. In school, they are already close. David, recalling the legendary Scheherazade, is to tell Steerforth stories morning and night, and Steerforth, to sooth David's throat, administers cowslip wine "through a piece of quill in the cork ... Sometimes, to make it a more sovereign specific, he was so kind as to squeeze orange juice into it, or to stir it up with ginger." When David sees Steerforth after many years, it is all he can do not to throw his arms around him. Instead, he weeps. To Steerforth, David is darling, little Daisy. To David, Steerforth is the god who can do no wrong. In David's company, Steerforth wants to be a better man. In their last scene together, he says, "Daisy, for though that's not the name your Godfathers and Godmothers gave you, it's the name I like best to call you by—and I wish, I wish, you could give it to me!" In the end, Steerforth's betrayal is more shattering than anything else in the book. And more poignant than Dora's death is Steerforth lying drowned on the shore—"among the ruins of the house he had wronged—I saw him lying with his head upon his arm, as I had often done in school."

DICKENS AND TONE

Even in its ending, *David Copperfield* is the sweetest of books; it is not surprising that many years later Dickens still called it his "favorite child." There is no unease at the end. The good end happily, and the bad end unhappily—David escapes undamaged and is as fresh as he was as a child, and Agnes has moved in to take over the duty of his permanent care. The novel has been accused, as has *Nicholas Nickleby*, of pandering to bourgeois values, with its marriage at the end, and compromise of its more interesting characters. Betsey Trotwood's property is reinstated, Micawber becomes a magistrate, and, indeed, the characters we love turn off their eccentricities and behave in a fashion that is disappointingly middle-class. But, in fact, such compromises are superceded by the book's innocence. It is, after all, a fairy tale, the work of a young man who is dreaming his life as it could have been.

Bleak House is not at all sweet, but angry—angrier even than the furious *Dombey and Son*, while grimmer than *Oliver Twist* and more effectively fierce than any book that was to come. (There is, in fact, so much fire that one of the characters dies of it—Mr. Krook spontaneously combusts.) It is perhaps the most daringly constructed of all Dickens novels. Gone are the odd, circus-like creatures that populate *The Old Curiosity Shop*; *Bleak House*'s freakish population is creepier because it is so much more real. Because we believe in bird-keeping old ladies and a desolate boy named Jo, in the end, we also believe in a London in which Mr. Krook can suddenly burst into flames. There are two narratives at work here—that of the grandiose, poetic, savage, and yet compassionate third-person narrator, who writes in the present tense, and the deeply personal, detailed recollections of Esther, who writes in the past tense. It is as if Dickens had separated his masculine and feminine sensibilities, elements that run most strongly in *David Copperfield*, distilled them, and divided them into two voices. The two narratives start out as quite disparate and gradually creep closer, until they echo and answer each other. For an author for whom plots are not a strength, the technique demonstrated in *Bleak House* is truly to be applauded.

Again, *Bleak House* is a work of anger. It is, after all, about a lawsuit that leaves in its wake death, madness, and ruination. Addiction—to the Court, to financial promise, to social propriety—is shown to be as poisonous as the addiction to opium that eventually takes Nemo's life. And London is a deadlier place than before, for it withers away good people. It is a place of barred windows, slime, and pauper graveyards. The characters in *Bleak House* are under a spell cast by the city, so it is appropriate that the third-person narrative often sounds like an incantation:

> Come night, come darkness, for you cannot come too soon, or stay too long, by such a place as this! ... Come, flame of gas, burning so sullenly above the iron gate, on which poisoned air deposits its witch-ointment slimy to the touch!

Still, just as Dickens loves his villains, so he loves London; it is still a circus, a festival. But gone is the joy that infects *The Old Curiosity Shop*.

This London is more sinister because it is more recognizable—a London inhabited by Kroop and Twite, as well as the ever-clamoring Jellybys and Mr. Turveytop.

The tone of *Bleak House* is best exemplified by one of its central characters, Jo; nowhere has London appeared to be so constantly alive, such a monster that consumes—and Jo, ultimately, is its most memorable victim.

> There he sits, the sun going down, the river running fast, the crowd flowing by him in two streams—everyone moving on to some purpose and to one end—until he is stirred up, and told to 'move on' too.

Jo is different from most of Dickens' other poor. He is not a prophet in misshapen guise, like Smike; nor an eloquent emblem, like Nancy; nor the Devil, like Fagin; nor the gentleman in beggar's clothes, like Oliver. He is merely an idiot boy, unclean and malodorous, and, unlike many poor characters, he does not charm. But he is a boy, and he is doomed. We are forced to watch every minute of Jo's short life, and in doing so we cringe. *Bleak House* is full of characters like Jo—but so was the real London. For in being unremarkable, he is familiar; his very ordinariness evokes outrage for other nameless faces ignored.

Jo also connects the social classes; he becomes the keystone that supports Krook, Nemo, Esther, and Lady Dedlock, and this role cements his importance as an embodiment of Dickens' relationship to his London. For *Bleak House* is Dickens' first attempt at social commentary. In it, classes merge. Esther and Ada sit in a hovel and witness a baby's death. Nemo expires in poverty, while his lover, Lady Dedlock, reigns in Lancashire and their illegitimate child, Esther, is at least cared for by the bourgeoisie. Class divisions are overcome by coincidence: Going to find Nemo's body, Lady Dedlock enlists Jo. Lady Dedlock and Esther come in contact via Mr. Jarndyce. Lady Dedlock dies spectacularly beside the unmarked tomb of her lover, dressed in her maid's clothes. Ultimately, the "good" people—at least those who remain—retreat from the courts and from London, from poverty and the aristocracy alike. Esther marries Allan Woodcourt, a doctor, and settles in Yorkshire. But her home, like her home before it, is called Bleak House. And both iterations of Bleak House, though cheerful in decor, will always recall the misery of their origins.

Indeed, tragedy typifies the tone of Bleak House and much of Dickens' other late work. Its plot could exist only in the romantic imagination, for *Bleak House* is still theater, though coincidence—the novelist's privilege—brings its characters together and drives the plot. But what rings true is Dickens' description of self-destructive human beings. Most of the characters in *Bleak House* who end badly are not blameless, but nor do they deserve their fate. Lord Dedlock, like Mr. Dombey from *Dombey and Son*, is felled by his pride; but unlike the cold, handsome-whiskered, entrepreneurial Dombey, he is a good man who loves his wife passionately. Similarly, cold Lady Dedlock, though as bored on the outside as Edith Dombey, is self-destructive within; but what rages in her breast is not the result of a hard heart, but a soft one— her passion for Nemo and the child it engendered. In *Bleak House*, good people do not necessarily end well. And some of the good people who emerge triumphant do not leave us cheering as heartily as we did in the past. Mr. Jarndyce is an example: We *should* love him as we love all other wise and cheerful benefactors. But there is something disquieting about Mr. Jarndyce. He is a jolly business man, but not cut from the same cloth as *Nicholas Nickleby*'s Brothers Cheeryble. He is, after all, the possessor of such an unlucky name, and he rules a house that is not so promisingly titled either. There is something unsettling about his decision to marry the 12-year-old Esther, and ultimately there is something chilling about his unsparing treatment of Richard—as becomes increasingly common in later Dickens.

REVERSALS OF CHARACTER IN THE LATER WORKS

Richard is likeable, and though Richard is mostly responsible for his own downfall, Mr. Jarndyce contributes to it through his lack of compassion. In Richard is demonstrated the darker counterpart to everything that we once considered good: like the young Dickensian heroes, Nicholas Nickleby and even David Copperfield, Richard has a sense of entitlement. He is out to seek his fortune and wants to find it quickly. Combined with his adoration of Ada, this makes him the brash, underpaid, charming, romantic young man who loves desperately, is loyal and prone to errors in judgement, and fancies himself the hero. Nicholas, like all the heroes after him, wins the girl *and* the fortune, but Richard, who is not the hero, dies when the girl is pregnant with his child, leaving her in poverty and heartbreak.

Then there is perhaps the most tingling of all Dickens' reversals of character. For Harold Skimpole, with his charm, his perpetual trouble with his creditors, and even in his affectations—is essentially a Mr. Micawber gone bad. Micawber affects the beaming countenance of the eccentric uncle, and Harold Skimpole affects the habits of the carefree child; but in most other aspects they are the same. They have large families, and are never more engaged than when they are occupied with some useless activity. They declare allegiance to love and irresponsibility. Later, Micawber will appear in the character of Mr. Dorrit, who is not a traitor like Skimpole, but in whom Micawber's grandiloquence and self-delusion are made pathetic. And above all, Skimpole, Mr. Dorrit, and Micawber are snobs. The Jellybys and Turveytops are humorous, but there is a harshness in their fun. We cannot distance ourselves from the fact that Mrs. Jellyby is a bad mother, or that Mr. Turveytop will slave poor Caddy and Prince to death. Dickens is older, sadder, and less in love with his "children"—like turning Mr. Micawber into Skimpole, he is letting them get away with less. Comedy is simply not present, and the compassion for the human condition that characterizes his earlier work begins to fade noticeably.

Still, in later Dickens there is more nonspecific hope—not of the sunny *David Copperfield* variety, but a hope that is more permanent. The hope represented by Amy and Arthur is muted, but also greater, because the world that they have overcome is darker. The same humane optimism that has run through Dickens' work still exists; it just has to struggle harder, and it is all the more gripping when it triumphs. It is interesting to note that *Bleak House*, though an angry book, avoids bitterness, with the help of Esther Summerson as narrator. *Little Dorrit*, though melancholy, is not despairing—yet Dickens' excessive genius seems distilled here, and one can posit with safety that this work marks an artistic deceleration. Readers are more reluctant to play into Dickens' more sentimental hand; still, for less elevated readers, his increased sentimental powers are impressive, and of a different order of brilliance. Above all, he is so skillful at eliciting tears; most do not cry over *Oliver Twist*, or even *The Old Curiosity Shop*, but many bawl over Lady Dedlock and Amy Dorrit. Victorians wept—even MacCauley and George Eliot are known to have indulged in tears. Dickens' later novels, unlike his earlier work, excite in their readers a more ready emotion. This brings us to *Great Expectations*.

GREAT EXPECTATIONS

Some consider it despicable (Margaret Oliphant called it "feeble ...
fatigued ... colorless"[9]), and others think it Dickens' most beautiful work.
It has been argued that his comic characters are the weakest here.
Dickens himself seems not enchanted by Uncle Pumblechook, the
conniving Sarah Pocket, or Mrs. Pocket. He sees through them, and he
writes them with a sort of cynicism missing from his earlier books. Mr.
Wopsle, however, the church clerk–turned–tormented actor, is pure
merriment, inciting a riot wherever he goes. Uncle Pumblechook,
though less lovable, is still funny; he is the rarest of Dickens creations, a
hypocrite—constantly extending his fat fingers to say, "May I? May I?"
Similarly, Sarah Pocket, with her pickled walnut face, is hilarious, as is
Mrs. Pocket, who as a mother is much more awful than Mrs. Jellyby.
This is comedy with a sting, and one could even call it cynicism. For we
are seeing these characters through Pip, and Pip is neither the sweet
Esther nor the starry-eyed David. He is acute, clever, sarcastic, flawed,
and deeply realistic.

　　While David is more awed by his own world, Pip's world is
certainly weirder. At its center reigns Miss Havisham, at once aristocrat
and ghoul. Her history does not match her sinister behavior; she was
only left at the altar, and though in Victorian England such a thing was
closer to catastrophe, her response is still extreme. But she lingers vividly
for us, frightening—her wedding dress, moth-eaten cake, stopped
clocks, and candlelit rooms. We can almost smell her decomposition,
and in the end, like a vampire, she vanishes into flames.

　　Then there are the good characters in *Great Expectations*, and
Dickens describes them with all the sentimental powers of his later
career. Witty Herbert Pocket is the perfect friend. Wemmick is comical
but too kind and efficient to rival the wackiness of some of the early
characters. While Mr. Micawber is completely out of character in
unveiling Uriah Heep, there is nothing out of character in Wemmick's
assisting Pip. In fact, he is Pip's most reliable ally, infinitely better in a
pinch than the scatterbrained Herbert. When the efficiency of his
professional life is united with the love in his domestic—when he acts
efficiently out of compassion—he is a valuable friend indeed.

　　But Pip is by far the most interesting. Even his name, Pip, conjures
an image of someone fresh, young, cheeky, full of promise. His voice is
self-assured and intentionally humorous. That Pip is imaginative is

certain. We meet him—much as we might imagine young Charles Dickens—conjuring physical pictures of his dead parents from their tombstone inscriptions, and of his five little brothers, to whom he feels "indebted for a belief I religiously entertained that they had all been born on their backs with their hands in their trousers pockets" because they had given up "trying to get a living exceedingly early in that universal struggle." As a child, David Copperfield captures the world from a perspective full of wonderment; Pip's narrative captures a boy's pop-eyed exaggeration. George Orwell says that the opening scene with Magwich is spoiled by its comedy,[10] but in fact the scene is a success, for it is quintessentially Pip:

> After each question he tilted me over a little more, so as to give me a greater sense of helplessness and danger.
> "You get me a file." He tilted me again. "And you get me wittles." He tilted me again. "You bring 'em both to me." He tilted me again. "Or I'll have your heart and liver out." He tilted me again.
> I was dreadfully frightened, and so giddy that I clung to him with both hands and said, "If you would kindly please to let me keep upright, sir, perhaps I shouldn't be sick, and perhaps I could attend more."

This is Dickens' tightest book; as an author he is confident as Pip. Every passage is alive, so packed with color and punch, they ring in our ears and eyeballs. However, we would not be surprised if Dickens himself preferred *David Copperfield*. David is dreamy, we cheer for his triumphs; Pip fills us with an acute sense of discomfort because he shows us a side of ourselves that we do not like. Pip is wittier than David, he is also less sweet. Even as a boy, he is suspicious of his aunt and her guests—he knows they belittle him, and that they are spiteful and pompous.

The comedy in the narrative never wanes, but it becomes darker, harder, fiercer, as Pip and his ambitions grow. Pip is Dickens most brilliantly rounded creation, his anti-hero. David, ambitious and earnest, realizes his ambitions and stays sweet; Pip, ambitious and earnest, realizes his ambitions and is spoiled. David calls one of his chapters "My First Dissipation," but the dissipation is never repeated; Pip in London is *perpetually* dissipated—he falls deeper into debt, pulls

Herbert, who cannot afford to be, in with him, joins a gentlemen's club, and spends most of his nights drunk and brawling. Though there is villainy in Orlick and in Arthur Compeyson, we never really recognize it; it is Pip who is his story's most compelling villain. In *Great Expectations*, loving, promising boys, when rewarded, do not necessarily develop into loving, promising young men.

The central discomfort in *Great Expectations* is that Pip does not deserve to be loved by those who love him; and betrays them by loving the one person who cannot love him in return. We know that Pip, in his pursuit of his expectations, will betray Joe, and it breaks our heart. Joe is loyal and husky and funny; we never tire of him. He is endowed with beautiful verbal powers, artless, vivid, and hilarious. Even his first words are poetry. "Mrs. Joe has been out a dozen times, looking for you, Pip. And she's out now, making it a baker's dozen." His actions, too, are poetic. As Pip tells us, "... he always aided and comforted me when he could, in some way of his own, and he always did so at dinner-time by giving me gravy; if there were any. There being plenty of gravy to-day, Joe spooned into my plate, at this point, about half a pint." Yet Joe is proud. This is not pride in the style of Mr. Dombey, or of Lord Dedlock; this is "simple dignity." Critics have called Joe a child, but this he is certainly not; he is a man, with, as Pip says, "a manly heart" despite his lack of education or manner. When Pip is taken from him, he stays away out of masculine self-respect. Squeezed into his "Sunday best," he issues a roundabout blessing:

> Pip, dear old chap, life is made of ever so many partings welded together, as I may say, and one man's a blacksmith, and one's a whitesmith, and one's a goldsmith, and one's a coppersmith. Diwisions among such must come, and must be met as they come. If there's been any fault at all today, it's mine. You and me is not two figures to be together in London, nor yet anywheres else but what is private, and beknown, and understood among friends. It ain't that I am proud, but that I want to be right, as you shall never see me no more in these clothes. I'm wrong in these clothes. I'm wrong out of the forge, the kitchen, or off th' meshes. You won't find half so much fault in me if you think of me in my forge dress, with my hammer in my hand, or even my pipe ... I'm awful dull, but I hope I've beat out something nigh the

rights of this at last. And so GOD bless you, dear old Pip, old chap, GOD bless you!

Dickens loves Joe here as unreservedly as he once loved Little Nell; unlike Nell, Joe is a triumph. It does not matter whether his "marsh" dialect is accurate, for it echoes when we read him. Joe makes us laugh, but with tears in our eyes.

But Pip, an orphan, has two fathers, Joe and Magwich. Dickens' underworld heroes have often been criticized—Nancy being in the forefront, the philosophical prostitute with the heart of gold. But Magwich is not a philosopher, he looks sinister and his habits are horrible, he smokes vile smelling tobacco and snaps up his food like "a hungry old dog." On him, we can still smell violence. "I've come to the old country fur to see my gentleman spend his money *like* a gentleman. That'll be *my* pleasure. My pleasure 'll be fur to see him do it. And blast you all!" And yet, Magwich is a hero; he becomes transfigured in his love for Pip; like a father who knows that his son is ashamed of him, he tries, for Pip's sake, not to "be low." Magwich, with dignity, takes his sentence at the dock, all the time holding Pip's hand. At the end it is Magwich's love, and not Joe's, that changes Pip. For Magwich sacrifices his own life for his love, and as he lies dying and condemned, Pip writes,

> ... now my repugnance to him had all melted away, and in the hunted wounded shackled creature who held my hand in his, I only saw a man who had meant to be my benefactor, and who had felt affectionately, gratefully, and generously towards me with great constancy through a series of years. I only saw in him a much better man than I had been to Joe.

Pip seems to surpass Nicholas and David, who emerge from their stories triumphant and ready to take the world, by decades. While not much older than either of them, he seems as old as Arthur Clenham, even before like Clenham he goes abroad. He has already had the world and been disappointed. Most of Dickens' heroes marry the quiet girls in the end—unions based on trust; but Pip does not marry Biddy, who meets the qualifications of the patient heroine. It is said that *Great Expectations* is Dickens' most unhappy book, but it is not, though it may be the saddest. The hope at the end of the book is in the small things: in love and loyalty and the sight of Joe at the hearth. It is a saddened hope,

but it is tempered and therefore enduring. To give it sweetness, there is
the comfort of knowing that Wemmick is happily settled in his little
castle with the green-gloved Miss Skiffin and his Aged Parent.

So *Great Expectations* ends happily, unless you take to heart
Dickens' revised ending, in which Pip ends up with Estella, and which
would make the work tragic indeed. As George Bernard Shaw says,
"Indeed, that anyone could have been happy with Estella, is positively
unpleasant."[11] Some find the character of Estella the most enticing of all
Dickens' creations, but not many; whereas most of Dickens' proud
women use pride to mask their emotional ferment, Estella is not prideful
but simply frozen. There is no capriciousness in her, no gaiety, no
contradiction, no fierceness, no depth. She doesn't, as does Edith
Dombey, even have the emotional capacity to feel wronged. In fact, she
is more weapon than woman. Presumably, some of her missing heart is
beaten into her through Bentley Drummle, but this is dubious. We
understand Pip's obsession with her; but Pip and Estella walking hand in
hand into the fog is Pip walking into eternal misery.

Nonetheless, the novel remains a celebration of human potential.
The faith in *Great Expectations* is stronger because the world is more
wicked. The portraits of London are less verbose than in his other
books, but in their brevity they are more gruesome. Smithfield is
"asmear with filth and blood and fat and foam." And at every moment,
it seems, someone is being hanged. There are the two death masks of
Mr. Jaggers, "peculiarly swollen and twitchy about the nose." Wemmick
is a good man, but terribly morbid, with his collection of portable
property willed to him by the condemned.

And surely nothing in all of Dickens is grimmer than the image of
"two-and-thirty men and women" sentenced to death at one time.
Hanging in Dickens' London is a business; property is exchanged,
shillings received for the giving of court tours, and the judge passes
group sentences so as not to make himself hoarse. And yet, amidst this,
the kindness of Joe endures. The passion of Magwich endures. Herbert
endures, and so does Wemmick. Wemmick marries, shortly after
Magwich is caught and before he is condemned, and in the cheeriness
that is the wedding party we see that little bright spark of human
kindness shining in the gloom. It is no stretch to think of Trabb's boy
mocking Pip as Pip walks down the street in his gentlemen's clothes, so
it is a testament to every man's potential when Trabb's boy saves Pip
from certain death.

In the end, *Great Expectations* is about one of Dickens' pet themes, in literature as in life: redemption. Magwich redeems himself, beautifully. Pip redeems himself by returning to Joe's hearth and ensuring Herbert's future. Says Miss Havisham, "If you can ever write under my name, 'I forgive her' ... pray do it!" And Pip does. For Miss Havisham in leaving her inheritance to Matthew and setting up Herbert in business, transcends those decades she spent in her brides dress, stewing in gall; she even redeems herself in the ruin of Pip and Estella. Estella, however dubiously, is redeemed. And so is the terrorizing Mrs. Joe, by one of the shortest and most poignant deathbed scenes that Dickens ever wrote. As recounted by Biddy, "And so presently she said 'Joe' again, and once 'Pardon' and once 'Pip.' And so she never lifted her head up any more ... " Then there is the genuinely astonishing surprise of Mr. Jaggers, who begins sinister, becomes more so, and then reveals himself as quite noble in the end. That a man like Mr. Jaggers is allowed to show his soft side makes this Dickens' most generous book. Ultimately, we, and Pip, have real faith—that lawyers like Jaggers have a heart, that Wemmick is divine, that friendship with a Herbert Pocket can transcend all the "portable property" in the world, and that even a virago like Mrs. Joe and an aberration like Miss Havisham can make this world a better place.

DICKENS AS SOCIAL CRITIC

There are many books written already about Dickens as a social critic— in *Great Expectations*, a boy escapes his calling as a blacksmith and goes off to be a gentleman; in *Bleak House*, all social classes are pulled together by one court case; in *Our Mutual Friend*, Dickens' last completed book, a pauper marries a gentleman and a gentleman becomes a pauper—but it is limiting to read Dickens only as such. *Bleak House* is an effective, absorbing, overwhelmingly angry book, but as a social critique it is unsuccessful; for (as many victims of his attacks have pointed out) Dickens invented too much about the court system and even the neighborhoods. *Hard Times* is more rigorous in its facts and more accurate in its critique, but *Hard Times* is far from being Dickens' best book.

Certainly, there are elements of the social critic in Dickens. He treats the poor with compassion. He made sure that there were cheap editions of his novels, and declined to give public readings unless there were seats which could be readily purchased by everyone. No one describes the clatter of street conversation more lyrically than Dickens, or elevates popular dialect more to poetry. Ultimately, however, the happiness that his heroes find is that of the middle class. Throughout his novels runs the paranoia that Dickens himself felt as a boy—of a shabby gentility's descent into anonymous poverty. David and Arthur and Esther don't want to be aristocrats, but nor do they want to be poor.

Moreover, all Dickens' *heroes* speak with the diction and accent of the genteel. This is not so difficult to accept in Nicholas Nickleby and David Copperfield, who at least originate, however distantly, in the better classes; but it is striking in the street-bred Oliver Twist. Oliver speaks nothing like Artful, or Fagin, or Bill Sikes; he speaks like Mr. Brownlow. Though Oliver turns out, ultimately, to be a gentleman's son, when he says, still ensconced in the work-house, "Please sir, I want some more," he is already, however, unconsciously, betraying his origins. There is Pip, who was brought up "by hand" by a blacksmith's wife. Pip's question to his elders, "I should like to know—if you wouldn't much mind—where the firing comes from," is of a completely different pedigree than the response, which details "conwicts" from "prison-ships, right 'cross th' meshes."

Even stranger is Lizzie Hexham in *Our Mutual Friend*. For though her father once robbed corpses, she says things like

> I have never dreamed of the possibility of his being anything to me on this earth but the kind picture that I know I could not make you understand ... [a]nd yet I love him. I love him so much, and so dearly, that when I sometimes think my life may be but a weary one, I am proud of it and glad of it.

Our Mutual Friend is the most socially radical of Dickens' novels, for in it the classes merge and remain merged. John Harmon, a gentleman, goes to work for his father's old servants. Lizzie loves another gentleman Eugene Wrayburn and will eventually marry him. However, if Lizzie talked like her father, it is quite possible that Eugene would have never been attracted to her in the first place, or at least would have never pursued her with ultimately noble motives in mind. Lizzie would have become another Nancy.

Apparently, then, the curse of the poor, expressed so ardently by Nancy and by Stephen Blackpool in *Hard Times*, is something that can be overcome through the modification of speech. The main characters, with their genteel diction, are socially mobile; their gentility is inherent. And just as the lower class should be revered, it is also a trap. Charles Dickens took the name of his only friend from his boyhood, Bob Fagin, for *Oliver Twist*'s villain. For just as Bob Fagin in life tried to acclimate Dickens to his poor circumstances, so does Bob Fagin in the book try to "break" Oliver. Dickens' own boyhood struggle with the shabby thing he called his gentility is evident; even in the worst circumstances, he seems to say, one should always remember who one is.

There are two types of gentility in Dickens' book—the gentility determined by rank and birth and the gentility that is intrinsic. It has been often said that, with the exception of Eugene Wrayburn, Dickens has never created a gentleman hero. Perhaps it is more appropriate to say that Eugene Wrayburn is Dickens' only elite hero. For *Nicholas Nickleby, David Copperfield, Great Expectations*, and other books are about becoming a gentleman in the most basic sense of the word—a gentle man. Pip, in his expectations, becomes a gentleman in demeanor, but not a gentleman in heart. He has to return to Joe to be truly gentlemanly. The mercenary Bella Wilfer—one of Dickens' more complex creations—cannot assume her rightful position as a gentlewoman until she has let go of her spite. Eugene Wrayburn, gentleman in status, does not become a real gentleman until he redeems himself with Lizzie Hexham, and Lizzie Hexham has always been suited to be his wife because she has a genteel soul.

THE LIFE AND THE WORK

The easy connections between social criticism and Dickens' England, and between Dickens' marriage and his portrayal of love, are irresistible. Dickens seems to have written himself into his books consistently—most notably he is David Copperfield, but he also can be found in characters as diverse as Dick Swiveller and Mr. Dick, who is writing a tract on King Charles. He also uses the names of women in his life—his wife (Kate), his gifted older sister (Fanny), and even, ultimately, his mistress (Ellen, in the name of Helena Landless). That a sister character should bear the name of his wife (as in the case of Kate Nickleby) is tantalizing, and certainly such instances support speculation on the nature of his neuroses. But to judge Dickens' work as a product of his neuroses does not give sufficient credit to his imagination. If we attribute all Dickens' proud, multifaceted women to the tutelage of Ellen Ternan, then we cannot account for Edith Dombey and Lady Dedlock.

David Copperfield is easy to read as autobiographical because in it Dickens appropriated long passages from his abandoned autobiography. But Dickens is an unreliable reporter. In his essay "Nurse's Stories" he writes about the tales spun by his nurse at bedtime—the captain, for instance, who used to file his teeth sharp and eat his brides chopped, salted, peppered, and baked in pies. For us, the essay reads as pure invention, but there is a good chance that Dickens probably believed in it himself. Dickens remembers his boyhood by *feeling* it through the vivid sensibilities of a child. Hence, the six most miserable months of his youth are consolidated—in Forster's interviews and in *David Copperfield*— into a few saturated sensations—the taste of beer on a birthday, a tiny plate of beef à la mode, the grim black letters of *COFFE ROOM* [sic] painted on the window but seen from inside to read *MOOR EFFOC*,[12] the wallpaper that he describes as "stenciled all over with an ornament that my young imagination represented as a blue muffin." The actual events are unimportant, and *MOOR EFFOC* and blue muffins loom large. Is Dickens David? Most assuredly. But the Dickens revived in the pages of the novel is not necessarily an accurate one, for *David Copperfield*, though autobiographical, is a "holiday." The suffering that Dickens must have experienced has no place. In *Copperfield*, Dickens has preferred to recount his boyhood as a daydream. It is telling that Dickens probably believed that David is more real than his actual young self. Edmund Wilson says, "If the novelist is extremely popular, he may even substitute his relation to his public for the ordinary human relations."[13] Dickens seems also to have substituted the relations that he created for his public for the ordinary human ones. Therefore, we can suggest that Ellen Ternan did not inspire all of those proud women with whose inspiration she is credited, as much as Estella and Helen and Bella inspired Dickens in inventing the recorded Ternan herself.

In this way, his private personality never contradicts his romantic hopefulness. Dickens was a man who was moved easily to anger and tears; loved his children but also made them wretched; humiliated his wife by moving out of their bedroom in front of the servants; and later said, upon leaving her, "I find that the skeleton in my domestic closet has become a pretty big one"—referring not only to his misery, but also to his wife's ever-expanding girth.[14] He preferred to be a public man, when he could shed the more ambiguous aspects of his personality, and was jolly and wonderful and charged. It is not surprising, then, that he should take so well to the stage and to public readings, for it was on the stage that he was most loved, and that he most loved himself.

There was no pettiness in the Dickens that clowned about under stage lights. Ultimately, he burned all his letters in 1860 because it was the petty aspects of his personality that he wished to hide. He had already explored his secret self—through his heroes and also his villains. His longing for Maria Beadnell was immortalized by David and Dora, and Arthur and Flora; his less savory longing for his young sister-in-law Mary Hogarth, the "third musketeer" to the early years of his marriage, was captured by Quilp's lust for little Nell. But personal probing was brilliant, entertaining, dramatic. Perhaps this was why he found his own marriage particularly distressing. Catherine Dickens was no shrew; nor was she an aloof goddess or foolish, babbling gossip—in short, she lacked the potential to become fictively grand. If she was anything like Agnes, then we can assume—which empirical evidence leads us to do anyway—that Dickens found her boring indeed. And while marriage is frequently miserable in Dickens' work, there is excitement even in that; but while marriage with Catherine might have been unhappy, there was just no greatness in it. It approached neither the magnificent destruction of the Dombeys nor the macabre household of the Quilps, nor yet the hopeless Pockets.

Even after separation from his wife, Dickens continued to love his children; and though he often made them sad, all of them, with the exception of the youngest, lived with him. On the stage and off, he was a father, and even more so, a child. For Dickens' world is a child's world, always bright, exciting, alive, interpreted with a sanity that is both inquisitive and naive. He experienced things as if for the first time, exaggerated eccentricities; surely, while writing Mr. Micawber he shared that man's delusions. A child's point of view redeems life itself. For young David Copperfield, one kindly tavern keeper is more memorable than the countless brutes and swindlers he has encountered on the street. While Dickens was never able to write many children with conviction, all his adults have a child's perspective. The most valuable redemption, even for grown-ups, is that of innocence; David never leaves it, Arthur discovers it in Amy Dorrit, and Pip must return to it.

To judge from his work, Dickens must have desired redemption poignantly, ardently, toward the end of his life. In *Our Mutual Friend*,

Bella, the corrupted Mr. Boffin, Lizzie Hexham, and Lizzie's father all find redemption. And despite the fact that he was exhausted and in many ways lovelorn, Dickens himself *was* redeemed—by an exquisite death. As if in anticipation, he had pronounced a farewell to his public not long before: "[F]rom these garish lights," he'd said, "I vanish now for ever more...."[15] On his last day, he apologized to his eldest daughter, Katey, wishing that he had been "a better father—a better man."[16] That night, he collapsed at the dinner table after writing an installment of *Edwin Drood*.

Somebody sent for a doctor, the messenger riding a pony named after a character in *Nicholas Nickleby*. In a move that Dickens could have written for himself, a tear trickled down his cheek just before the end. His last words: "Yes, on the ground."

He could not have wished for a better way to leave the stage.

Notes

1. Henry James, "On *Our Mutual Friend*," also called, "The Limitations of Dickens," for the Nation, reprinted in *The Dickens Critics*, Cornell University Press, pp. 48–54.

2. John Forster, in an unsigned review of Nicholas Nickleby for the Examiner, reprinted in *Dickens: The Critical Heritage*, 50.

3. Anonymous, in an unsigned piece, 'Dickens and his Works,' reprinted in *Dickens: A Critical Heritage*, 90.

4. Angus Wilson, introduction, *The Mystery of Edwin Drood*, Penguin Books, 1974, p. 10.

5. G.K. Chesterton, *Charles Dickens*, pp. 46-7.

6. Jack Lindsay, *Dickens*, pp. 192, 199.

7. Peter Ackroyd, *Dickens*, 823; also cited in numerous other biographies.

8. Claire Tomalin, *The Invisible Woman*, 85.

9. Margaret Oliphant, from 'Sensation Novels,' reprinted in *Charles Dickens: A Critical Anthology*, 159.

10. George Orwell, "Charles Dickens," in *The Dickens Critics*, pp. 162-3. He writes, "although the speech shows a remarkable knowledge of the way in which a child's mind works, its actual words are...out of tune with what is to follow."

11. George Bernard Shaw, "Preface to Great Expectations," in *Charles Dickens: A Critical Anthology*, 294.

12. John Forster, *Life of Charles Dickens*, 28.
13. Edmund Wilson, "The Two Scrooges," in *Wound and the Bow*, 70.
14. Forster, *Life*, 639.
15. Ackroyd, *Dickens*, 1067, cited in numerous biographies and essays.
16. Ackroyd, *Dickens*, 1075, cited in numerous biographies.

WORKS CITED

Ackroyd, Peter. *Dickens*. New York: HarperCollins, 1990.
Cooper, Lettice Ulpha. *A Hand Upon the Time: A Life of Charles Dickens*. New York: Pantheon, 1968.
Dickens, Charles. *A Christmas Carol*. New York: Garden City, 1938.
———. *David Copperfield*. New York: Dodd Mead & Co., 1984.
———. *Dombey and Son*. New York: Dodd Mead & Son, 1950.
———. *The Old Curiosity Shop*. Pleasantville, New York: Reader's Digest Association, 1988.
———. *Pickwick Papers*. London and New York: McMillan & Co., Ltd., 1899.
———. *Sketches by Boz*. Everyman's Library. New York: Dutton, 1968.
Dudgeon, Piers. *Dickens' London*. London: Headline, 1987.
Forster, John. *The Life of Charles Dickens*. New York: Charles Scribner & Son, 1905.
Guide, Fred. *A Christmas Carol and its Adaptations*. Jefferson City, North Carolina: McFarland & Co., 2000.
Johnson, Edgar. *Charles Dickens: His Tragedy and Triumph*. New York: Simon & Schuster, 1952.
MacKenzie, Norman, Jeanne MacKenzie. *Dickens: A Life*. New York: Oxford University Press, 1979.
Schlicke, Paul, ed. *The Oxford Reader's Companion to Dickens*. New York: Oxford University Press, 1999.
Schwarzbach, F.S. *Dickens and the City*. London: University of London, Athlone Press, 1979.

HENRY JAMES

The Limitations of Dickens

Our Mutual Friend is, to our perception, the poorest of Mr. Dickens's works. And it is poor with the poverty not of momentary embarrassment, but of permanent exhaustion. It is wanting in inspiration. For the last ten years it has seemed to us that Mr. Dickens has been unmistakeably forcing himself. *Bleak House* was forced; *Little Dorrit* was laboured; the present work is dug out as with a spade and pickaxe.

Of course—to anticipate the usual argument—who but Dickens could have written it? Who, indeed? Who else would have established a lady in business in a novel on the admirably solid basis of her always putting on gloves and tying a handkerchief around her head in moments of grief, and of her habitually addressing her family with "Peace! hold!" It is needless to say that Mrs. Reginald Wilfer is first and last the occasion of considerable true humour. When, after conducting her daughter to Mrs. Boffin's carriage, in sight of all the envious neighbours, she is described as enjoying her triumph during the next quarter of an hour by airing herself on the doorstep "in a kind of splendidly serene trance," we laugh with as uncritical a laugh as could be desired of us. We pay the same tribute to her assertions, as she narrates the glories of the society she enjoyed at her father's table, that she has known as many as three copper-plate engravers exchanging the most exquisite sallies and retorts there at one time. But when to these we have added a dozen more

From *The Nation*, 1 (1865), 786–787 reprinted in *The Dickens Critics*, edited by George H. Ford and Lauriat Lane, Jr., Cornell University Press, 1961, pp. 48–54. Reprinted by permission.

happy examples of the humour which was exhaled from every line of Mr. Dickens's earlier writings, we shall have closed the list of the merits of the work before us.

To say that the conduct of the story, with all its complications, betrays a long-practised hand, is to pay no compliment worthy the author. If this were, indeed, a compliment, we should be inclined to carry it further, and congratulate him on his success in what we should call the manufacture of fiction; for in so doing we should express a feeling that has attended us throughout the book. Seldom, we reflected, had we read a book so intensely *written*, so little seen, known, or felt.

In all Mr. Dickens's works the fantastic has been his great resource; and while his fancy was lively and vigorous it accomplished great things. But the fantastic, when the fancy is dead, is a very poor business. The movement of Mr. Dickens's fancy in Mr. Wilfer and Mr. Boffin and Lady Tippins, and the Lammles and Miss Wren, and even in Eugene Wrayburn, is, to our mind, a movement lifeless, forced, mechanical. It is the letter of his old humour without the spirit. It is hardly too much to say that every character here put before us is a mere bundle of eccentricities, animated by no principle of nature whatever.

In former days there reigned in Mr. Dickens's extravagances a comparative consistency; they were exaggerated statements of types that really existed. We had, perhaps, never known a Newman Noggs, nor a Pecksniff, nor a Micawber; but we had known persons of whom these figures were but the strictly logical consummation. But among the grotesque creatures who occupy the pages before us, there is not one whom we can refer to as an existing type. In all Mr. Dickens's stories, indeed, the reader has been called upon, and has willingly consented, to accept a certain number of figures or creatures of pure fancy, for this was the author's poetry. He was, moreover, always repaid for his concession by a peculiar beauty or power in these exceptional characters. But he is now expected to make the same concession, with a very inadequate reward.

What do we get in return for accepting Miss Jenny Wren as a possible person? This young lady is the type of a certain class of characters of which Mr. Dickens has made a specialty, and with which he has been accustomed to draw alternate smiles and tears, according as he pressed one spring or another. But this is very cheap merriment and very cheap pathos. Miss Jenny Wren is a poor little dwarf, afflicted as she constantly reiterates, with a "bad back" and "queer legs," who makes doll's dresses, and is for ever pricking at those with whom she converses in the air, with her needle, and assuring them that she knows their "tricks and their manners." Like all Mr. Dickens's pathetic characters, she is a little monster; she is deformed, unhealthy, unnatural; she belongs to the troop of hunchbacks, imbeciles, and precocious children who have carried on the sentimental business in all Mr. Dickens's novels; the little Nells, the Smikes, the Paul Dombeys.

Mr. Dickens goes as far out of the way for his wicked people as he does for his good ones. Rogue Riderhood, indeed, in the present story, is villainous with a sufficiently natural villainy; he belongs to that quarter of society in which the author is most at his ease. But was there ever such wickedness as that of the Lammles and Mr. Fledgeby? Not that people have not been as mischievous as they; but was any one ever mischievous in that singular fashion? Did a couple of elegant swindlers ever take such particular pains to be aggressively inhuman?—for we can find no other word for the gratuitous distortions to which they are subjected. The word *humanity* strikes us as strangely discordant, in the midst of these pages; for, let us boldly declare it, there is no humanity here.

Humanity is nearer home than the Boffins, and the Lammles, and the Wilfers, and the Veneerings. It is in what men have in common with each other, and not what they have in distinction. The people just named have nothing in common with each other, except the fact that they have nothing in common with mankind at large. What a world were this world if the world of *Our Mutual Friend* were an honest reflection of it! But a community of eccentrics is impossible. Rules alone are consistent with each other; exceptions are inconsistent. Society is maintained by natural sense and natural feeling. We cannot conceive a society in which these principles are not in some manner represented. Where in these pages are the depositaries of that intelligence without which the movement of life would cease? Who represents nature?

Accepting half of Mr. Dickens's persons as intentionally grotesque, where are those exemplars of sound humanity who should afford us the proper measure of their companions' variations? We ought not, in justice to the author, to seek them among his weaker—that is, his mere conventional—characters; in John Harmon, Lizzie Hexam, or Mortimer Lightwood; but we assuredly cannot find them among his stronger— that is, his artificial creations.

Suppose we take Eugene Wrayburn and Bradley Headstone. They occupy a half-way position between the habitual probable of nature and the habitual impossible of Mr. Dickens. A large portion of the story rests upon the enmity borne by Headstone to Wrayburn, both being in love with the same woman. Wrayburn is a gentleman, and Headstone is one of the people. Wrayburn is well-bred, careless, elegant, sceptical, and idle: Headstone is a high-tempered, hard-working, ambitious young schoolmaster. There lay in the opposition of these two characters a very good story. But the prime requisite was that they should *be* characters: Mr. Dickens, according to his usual plan, has made them simply figures, and between them the story that was to be, the story that should have been, has evaporated. Wrayburn lounges about with his hands in his pockets, smoking a cigar, and talking nonsense. Headstone strides about, clenching his fists and biting his lips and grasping his stick.

There is one scene in which Wrayburn chaffs the schoolmaster with easy insolence, while the latter writhes impotently under his well-bred sarcasm. This scene is very clever, but it is very insufficient. If the majority of readers were not so very timid in the use of words we should call it vulgar. By this we do not mean to indicate the conventional impropriety of two gentlemen exchanging lively personalities; we mean to emphasise the essentially small character of these personalities. In other words, the moment, dramatically, is great, while the author's conception is weak. The friction of two *men*, of two characters, of two passions, produces stronger sparks than Wrayburn's boyish repartees and Headstone's melodramatic commonplaces.

Such scenes as this are useful in fixing the limits of Mr. Dickens's insight. Insight is, perhaps, too strong a word; for we are convinced that it is one of the chief conditions of his genius not to see beneath the surface of things. If we might hazard a definition of his literary character, we should, accordingly, call him the greatest of superficial novelists. We are aware that this definition confines him to an inferior rank in the department of letters which he adorns; but we accept this consequence of our proposition. It were, in our opinion, an offence against humanity to place Mr. Dickens among the greatest novelists. For, to repeat what we have already intimated, he has created nothing but figure. He has added nothing to our understanding of human character. He is master of but two alternatives: he reconciles us to what is commonplace, and he reconciles us to what is odd. The value of the former service is questionable; and the manner in which Mr. Dickens performs it sometimes conveys a certain impression of charlatanism. The value of the latter service is incontestable, and here Mr. Dickens is an honest, an admirable artist.

But what is the condition of the truly great novelist? For him there are no alternatives, for him there are no oddities, for him there is nothing outside of humanity. He cannot shirk it; it imposes itself upon him. For him alone, therefore, there is a true and a false; for him alone, it is possible to be right, because it is possible to be wrong. Mr. Dickens is a great observer and a great humourist, but he is nothing of a philosopher.

Some people may hereupon say, so much the better; we say, so much the worse. For a novelist very soon has need of a little philosophy. In treating of Micawber, and Boffin, and Pickwick, *et hoc genus omne*, he can, indeed, dispense with it, for this—we say it with all deference—is not serious writing. But when he comes to tell the story of a passion, a story like that of Headstone and Wrayburn, he becomes a moralist as well as an artist. He must know *man* as well as *men*, and to know man is to be a philosopher.

The writer who knows men alone, if he have Mr. Dickens's humour and fancy, will give us figures and pictures for which we cannot be too grateful, for he will enlarge our knowledge of the world. But when he introduces men and women whose interest is preconceived to lie not in the poverty, the weakness, the drollery of their natures, but in their complete and unconscious subjection to ordinary and healthy human emotions, all his humour, all his fancy, will avail him nothing if, out of the fullness of his sympathy, he is unable to prosecute those generalisations in which alone consists the real greatness of a work of art.

This may sound like very subtle talk about a very simple matter. It is rather very simple talk about a very subtle matter. A story based upon those elementary passions in which alone we seek the true and final manifestation of character must be told in a spirit of intellectual superiority to those passions. That is, the author must understand what he is talking about. The perusal of a story so told is one of the most elevating experiences within the reach of the human mind. The perusal of a story which is not so told is infinitely depressing and unprofitable.

G. K. CHESTERTON

On the Alleged Optimism of Dickens

In one of the plays of the decadent period, an intellectual expressed the atmosphere of his epoch by referring to Dickens as "a vulgar optimist." I have in a previous chapter suggested something of the real strangeness of such a term. After all, the main matter of astonishment (or rather of admiration) is that optimism should be vulgar. In a world in which physical distress is almost the common lot, we actually complain that happiness is too common. In a world in which the majority is physically miserable we actually complain of the sameness of praise: we are bored with the abundance of approval. When we consider what the conditions of the vulgar really are, it is difficult to imagine a stranger or more splendid tribute to humanity than such a phrase as vulgar optimism. It is as if one spoke of "vulgar martyrdom" or "common crucifixion."

First, however, let it be said frankly that there is a foundation for the charge against Dickens which is implied in the phrase about vulgar optimism. It does not concern itself with Dickens' confidence in the value of existence and the intrinsic victory of virtue; that is not optimism but religion. It is not concerned with his habit of making bright occasions bright, and happy stories happy; that is not optimism, but literature. Nor is it concerned even with his peculiar genius for the description of an almost bloated joviality; that is not optimism, it is simply Dickens. With all these higher variations of optimism I deal

From *Charles Dickens*, House of Stratus, London, pp. 115–126 © 2001 by the Royal Literary Fund. Reprinted by permission.

elsewhere. But over and above all these there is a real sense in which Dickens laid himself open to the accusation of a vulgar optimism, and I desire to put the admission of this first, before the discussion that follows. Dickens did have a disposition to make his characters at all costs happy, or, to speak more strictly, he had a disposition to make them comfortable rather than happy. He had a sort of literary hospitality; he too often treated his characters as if they were his guests. From a host is always expected, and always ought to be expected as long as human civilization is healthy, a strictly physical benevolence, if you will, a kind of coarse benevolence. Food and fire and such things should always be the symbols of the man entertaining men; because they are the things which all men beyond question have in common. But something more than this is needed from the man who is imagining and making men, the artist, the man who is not receiving men, but rather sending them forth.

As I shall remark in a moment in the matter of the Dickens villains, it is not true that he made every one thus at home. But he did do it to a certain wide class of incongruous characters; he did it to all who had been in any way unfortunate. It had indeed its origin (a very beautiful origin) in his realization of how much a little pleasure was to such people. He knew well that the greatest happiness that has been known since Eden is the happiness of the unhappy. So far he is admirable. And as long as he was describing the ecstasy of the poor, the borderland between pain and pleasure, he was at his highest. Nothing that has ever been written about human delights, no Earthly Paradise, no Utopia has ever come so near the quick nerve of happiness as his descriptions of the rare extravagances of the poor; such an admirable description, for instance, as that of Kit Nubbles taking his family to the theatre. For he seizes on the real source of the whole pleasure; a holy fear. Kit tells the waiter to bring the beer. And the waiter, instead of saying, "Did you address that language to me," said, "Pot of beer, sir; yes, sir." That internal and quivering humility of Kit is the only way to enjoy life or banquets; and the fear of the waiter is the beginning of dining. People in this mood "take their pleasures sadly;" which is the only way of taking them at all.

So far Dickens is supremely right. As long as he was dealing with such penury and such festivity his touch was almost invariably sure. But when he came to more difficult cases, to people who for one reason or another could not be cured with one good dinner, he did develop this other evil, this genuinely vulgar optimism of which I speak. And the mark of it is this: that he gave the characters a comfort that had no especial connection with themselves; he threw comfort at them like alms. There are cases at the end of his stories in which his kindness to his characters is a careless and insolent kindness. He loses his real charity and adopts the charity of the Charity Organization Society; the charity that is not kind, the charity that is puffed up, and that does behave itself unseemly. At the end of some of his stories he deals out his characters a kind of out-door relief.

I will give two instances. The whole meaning of the character of Mr Micawber is that a man can be always almost rich by constantly expecting riches. The lesson is a really important one in our sweeping modern sociology. We talk of the man whose life is a failure; but Micawber's life never is a failure, because it is always a crisis. We think constantly of the man who if he looked back would see that his existence was unsuccessful; but Micawber never does look back; he always looks forward, because the bailiff is coming tomorrow. You cannot say he is defeated, for his absurd battle never ends; he cannot despair of life, for he is so much occupied in living. All this is of immense importance in the understanding of the poor; it is worth all the slum novelists that ever insulted democracy. But how did it happen, how could it happen, that the man who created this Micawber could pension him off at the end of the story and make him a successful colonial mayor? Micawber never did succeed, never ought to succeed; his kingdom is not of this world. But this is an excellent instance of Dickens' disposition to make his characters grossly and incongruously comfortable. There is another instance in the same book. Dora, the first wife of David Copperfield, is a very genuine and amusing figure; she has certainly far more force of character than Agnes. She represents the infinite and divine irrationality of the human heart. What possessed Dickens to make her such a dehumanized prig as to recommend her husband to marry another woman? One could easily respect a husband who after time and development made such a marriage, but surely not a wife who desired it. If Dora had died hating Agnes we should know that everything is wrong, at least if hypocrisy and artificiality and moral vulgarity are wrong. There, again, Dickens yields to a mere desire to give comfort. He wishes to pile up pillows round Dora; and he smothers her with them, like Othello.

This is the real vulgar optimism of Dickens; it does exist, and I have deliberately put it first. Let us admit that Dickens' mind was far too much filled with pictures of satisfaction and cosiness and repose. Let us admit that he thought principally of the pleasures of the oppressed classes; let us admit that it hardly cost him any artistic pang to make out human beings as much happier than they are. Let us admit all this, and a curious fact remains.

For it was this too easily contented Dickens, this man with cushions at his back and (it sometimes seems) cotton wool in his ears, it was this happy dreamer, this vulgar optimist who alone of modern writers did really destroy some of the wrongs he hated and bring about some of the reforms he desired. Dickens did help to pull down the debtors' prisons; and if he was too much of an optimist he was quite enough of a destroyer. Dickens did drive Squeers out of his Yorkshire den; and if Dickens was too contented, it was more than Squeers was. Dickens did leave his mark on parochialism, on nursing, on funerals, on public executions, on workhouses, on the Court of Chancery. These things were altered; they are different. It may be that such reforms are not adequate remedies: that is another question altogether. The next sociologists may think these old Radical reforms quite narrow or accidental. But such as they were, the old radicals got them done; and the new sociologists cannot get anything done at all. And in the practical doing of them Dickens played a solid and quite demonstrable part; that is the plain matter that concerns us here. If Dickens was an optimist he was an uncommonly active and useful kind of optimist. If Dickens was a sentimentalist he was a very practical sentimentalist.

And the reason of this is one that goes deep into Dickens' social reform, and like every other real and desirable thing, involves a kind of mystical contradiction. If we are to save the oppressed, we must have two apparently antagonistic emotions in us at the same time. We must think the oppressed man intensely miserable, and at the same time intensely attractive and important. We must insist with violence upon his degradation; we must insist with the same violence upon his dignity. For if we relax by one inch the one assertion, men will say he does not need saving. And if we relax by one inch the other assertion, men will say he is not worth saving. The optimists will say that reform is needless. The pessimists will say that reform is hopeless. We must apply both simultaneously to the same oppressed man; we must say that he is a worm and a god; and we must thus lay ourselves open to the accusation (or the compliment) of transcendentalism. This is, indeed, the strongest argument for the religious conception of life. If the dignity of man is an earthly dignity we shall be tempted to deny his earthly degradation. If it is a heavenly dignity we can admit the earthly degradation with all the candour of Zola. If we are idealists about the other world we can be realists about this world. But that is not here the point. What is quite evident is that if a logical praise of the poor man is pushed too far, and if a logical distress about him is pushed too far, either will involve wreckage to the central paradox of reform. If the poor man is made too admirable he ceases to be pitiable; if the poor man is made too pitiable he becomes merely contemptible. There is a school of smug optimists who will deny that he is a poor man. There is a school of scientific pessimists who will deny that he is a man.

Out of this perennial contradiction arises the fact that there are always two types of the reformer. The first we may call for convenience the pessimistic, the second the optimistic reformer. One dwells upon the fact that souls are lost; the other dwells upon the fact that they are worth saving. Both, of course, are (so far as that is concerned) quite right, but they naturally tend to a difference of method, and sometimes to a difference of perception. The pessimistic reformer points out the good elements that oppression has destroyed; the optimistic reformer, with an even fiercer joy, points out the good elements that it has not destroyed. It is the case for the first reformer that slavery has made men slavish. It is the case for the second reformer that slavery has not made men slavish. The first describes how bad men are under bad conditions. The second describes how good men are under bad conditions. Of the first class of writers, for instance, is Gorky. Of the second class of writers is Dickens.

But here we must register a real and somewhat startling fact. In the face of all apparent probability, it is certainly true that the optimistic reformer reforms much more completely than the pessimistic reformer. People produce violent changes by being contented, by being far too contented. The man who said that "revolutions are not made with rose-water" was obviously inexperienced in practical human affairs. Men like Rousseau and Shelley do make revolutions, and do make them with rose-water; that is, with a too rosy and sentimental view of human goodness. Figures that come before and create convulsion and change (for instance, the central figure of the New Testament) always have the air of walking in an unnatural sweetness and calm. They give us their peace ultimately in blood and battle and division; not as the world giveth give they unto us.

Nor is the real reason of the triumph of the too-contented reformer particularly difficult to define. He triumphs because he keeps alive in the human soul an invincible sense of the living being worth doing, of the war being worth winning, of the people being worth their deliverance. I remember that Mr William Archer, some time ago, published in one of his interesting series of interviews, an interview with Mr Thomas Hardy. That powerful writer was represented as saying, in the course of the conversation, that he did not wish at the particular moment to define his position with regard to the ultimate problem of whether life itself was worth living. There are, he said, hundreds of remediable evils in this world. When we have remedied all these (such was his argument), it will be time enough to ask whether existence itself, under its best possible conditions is valuable or desirable. Here we have presented, with a considerable element of what can only be called unconscious humour, the plain reason of the failure of the pessimist as a reformer. Mr Hardy is asking us, I will not say to buy a pig in a poke; he is asking us to buy a poke on the remote chance of there being a pig in it. When we have for some few frantic centuries tortured ourselves to save mankind, it will then be "time enough" to discuss whether they can possibly be saved. When, in the case of infant mortality, for example, we have exhausted ourselves with the earth-shaking efforts required to save the life of every individual baby, it will then be time enough to consider whether every individual baby would not have been happier dead. We are to remove mountains and bring the millennium, because then we can have a quiet moment to discuss whether the millennium is at all desirable. Here we have the low-water mark of the impotence of the sad reformer. And here we have the reason of the paradoxical triumph of the happy one. His triumph is a religious triumph; it rests upon his perpetual assertion of the value of the human soul and of human daily life. It rests upon his assertion that human life is enjoyable because it is human. And he will never admit, like so many compassionate pessimists, that human life ever ceases to be human. He does not merely pity the lowness of men; he feels an insult to their elevation. Brute pity should be given only to the brutes. Cruelty to animals is cruelty and a vile thing; but cruelty to a man is not cruelty, it is treason. Tyranny over a man is not tyranny, it is rebellion, for man is royal. Now, the practical weakness of the vast mass of modern pity for the poor and the oppressed is precisely that it is merely pity; the pity is pitiful, but not respectful. Men feel that the cruelty to the poor is a kind of cruelty to animals. They never feel that it is injustice to equals; nay, it is treachery to comrades. This dark, scientific pity, this brutal pity, has an elemental sincerity of its own; but it is entirely useless for all ends of social reform. Democracy swept Europe with the sabre when it was founded upon the Rights of Man. It has done literally nothing at all since it has been founded only upon the wrongs of man. Or, more strictly speaking, its recent failure has been due to its not admitting the existence of any rights or wrongs, or indeed of any humanity. Evolution (the sinister enemy of revolution) does not especially deny the existence of God; what it does deny is the existence of man. And all the despair about the poor, and the cold and repugnant pity for them, has been largely due to the vague sense that they have literally relapsed into the state of the lower animals.

A writer sufficiently typical of recent revolutionism—Gorky—has called one of his books by the eerie and effective title *Creatures that once were Men*. That title explains the whole failure of the Russian revolution. And the reason why the English writers, such as Dickens, did with all their limitations achieve so many of the actual things at which they aimed, was that they could not possibly have put such a title upon a human book. Dickens really helped the unfortunate in the matters to which he set himself. And the reason is that across all his books and sketches about the unfortunate might be written the common title, *Creatures that Still are Men*.

There does exist, then, this strange optimistic reformer; the man whose work begins with approval and yet ends with earthquake. Jesus Christ was destined to found a faith which made the rich poorer and the poor richer; but even when he was going to enrich them, he began with the phrase, "Blessed are the poor." The Gissings and the Gorkys say, as an universal literary motto, "Cursed are the poor." Among a million who have faintly followed Christ in this divine contradiction, Dickens stands out especially. He said, in all his reforming utterances, "Cure poverty;" but he said in all his actual descriptions, "Blessed are the poor." He described their happiness, and men rushed to remove their sorrow. He described them as human, and men resented the insults to their humanity. It is not difficult to see why, as I said at an earlier stage of this book, Dickens' denunciations have had so much more practical an effect than the determinations of such a man as Gissing. Both agreed that the souls of the people were in a kind of prison. But Gissing said that the prison was full of dead souls. Dickens said that the prison was full of living souls. And the fiery cavalcade of rescuers felt that they had not come too late.

Of this general fact about Dickens' descriptions of poverty there will not, I suppose, be any serious dispute. The dispute will only be about the truth of those descriptions. It is clear that whereas Gissing would say, "See how their poverty depresses the Smiths or the Browns," Dickens says, "See how little, after all, their poverty can depress the Cratchits." No one will deny that he made a special feature a special study of the subject of the festivity of the poor. We will come to the discussion of the veracity of these scenes in a moment. It is here sufficient to register in conclusion of our examination of the reforming optimist, that Dickens certainly was such an optimist, and that he made it his business to insist upon what happiness there is in the lives of the unhappy. His poor man is always a Mark Tapley, a man the optimism of whose spirit increases if anything with the pessimism of his experience. It can also be registered as a fact equally solid and quite equally demonstrable that this optimistic Dickens did effect great reforms.

The reforms in which Dickens was instrumental were indeed, from the point of view of our sweeping social panaceas, special and limited. But perhaps, for that reason especially, they afford a compact and concrete instance of the psychological paradox of which we speak. Dickens did definitely destroy—or at the very least help to destroy— certain institutions; he destroyed those institutions simply by describing them. But the crux and peculiarity of the whole matter is this, that, in a sense, it can really be said that he described these things too optimistically. In a real sense, he described Dotheboys Hall as a better place than it is. In a real sense, he made out the workhouse as a pleasanter place than it can ever be. For the chief glory of Dickens is that he made these places interesting; and the chief infamy of England is that it has made these places dull. Dullness was the one thing that Dickens' genius could never succeed in describing; his vitality was so violent that he could not introduce into his books the genuine impression even of a moment of monotony. If there is anywhere in his novels an instant of silence, we only hear more clearly the hero whispering with the heroine, the villain sharpening his dagger, or the creaking of the machinery that is to give out the god from the machine. He could splendidly describe gloomy places, but he could not describe dreary places. He could describe miserable marriages, but not monotonous marriages. It must have been genuinely entertaining to be married to Mr Quilp. This sense of a still incessant excitement he spreads over every inch of his story, and over every dark tract of his landscape. His idea of a desolate place is a place where anything can happen; he has no idea of that desolate place where nothing can happen. This is a good thing for his soul, for the place where nothing can happen is hell. But still, it might reasonably he maintained by the modern mind that he is hampered in describing human evil and sorrow by this inability to imagine tedium, this dullness in the matter of dullness. For, after all, it is certainly true that the worst part of the lot of the unfortunate is the fact that they have long spaces in which to review the irrevocability of their doom. It is certainly true that the worst days of the oppressed man are the nine days out of ten in which he is not oppressed. This sense of sickness and sameness Dickens did certainly fail or refuse to give. When we read such a description as that excellent one—in detail—of Dotheboys Hall, we feel that, while everything else is accurate, the author does, in the words of the excellent Captain Nares in Stevenson's *Wrecker*, "draw the dreariness rather mild." The boys at Dotheboys were, perhaps, less bullied, but they were certainly more bored. For, indeed, how could anyone be bored with the society of so sumptuous a creature as Mr Squeers? Who would not put up with a few illogical floggings in order to enjoy the conversation of a man who could say, "She's a rum 'un is Natur' ... Natur', is more easier conceived than described." The same principle applies to the workhouse in *Oliver Twist*. We feel vaguely that neither Oliver nor anyone else could be entirely unhappy in the presence of the purple personality of Mr Bumble. The one thing he did not describe in any of the abuses he denounced was the soul-destroying potency of routine. He made out the bad school, the bad parochial system, the bad debtor's prison as very much jollier and more exciting than they may really have been. In a sense, then, he flattered them; but he destroyed them with the flattery. By making Mrs Gamp delightful he made her impossible. He gave every one an interest in Mr Bumble's existence; and by the same act gave every one an interest in his destruction. It would be difficult to find a stronger instance of the futility and energy of the method which we have, for the sake of argument, called the method of the optimistic reformer. As long as low Yorkshire schools were entirely colourless and dreary, they continued quietly tolerated by the public, and quietly intolerable to the victims. So long as Squeers was dull as well as cruel he was permitted; the moment he became amusing as well as cruel he was destroyed. As long as Bumble was merely human he was allowed. When he became human, humanity wiped him out. For in order to do these great acts of justice we must always realize not only the humanity of the oppressed, but even the humanity of the oppressor. The satirist had, in a sense, to create the images in the mind before, as an iconoclast, he could destroy them. Dickens had to make Squeers live before he could make him die.

In connection with the accusation of vulgar optimism, which I have taken as a text for this chapter, there is another somewhat odd thing to notice. Nobody in the world was ever less optimistic than Dickens in his treatment of evil or the evil man. When I say optimistic in this matter I mean optimism in the modern sense, of an attempt to whitewash evil. Nobody ever made less attempt to whitewash evil than Dickens. Nobody black was ever less white than Dickens' black. He painted his villains and lost characters more black than they really are. He crowds his stories with a kind of villain rare in modern fiction—the villain really without any "redeeming point." There is no redeeming point in Squeers, or in Monks, or in Ralph Nickleby, or in Bill Sikes, or in Quilp, or in Brass, or in Mr. Chester, or in Mr. Pecksniff, or in Jonas Chuzzlewit, or in Carker, or in Uriah Heep, or in Blandois, or in a hundred more. So far as the balance of good and evil in human characters is concerned, Dickens certainly could not he called a vulgar optimist. His emphasis on evil was melodramatic. He might be called a vulgar pessimist.

Some will dismiss this lurid villainy as a detail of his artificial romance. I am not inclined to do so. He inherited, undoubtedly, this unqualified villain as he inherited so many other things, from the whole history of European literature. But he breathed into the blackguard a peculiar and vigorous life of his own. He did not show any tendency to modify his blackguardism in accordance with the increasing considerateness of the age; he did not seem to wish to make his villain less villainous; he did not wish to imitate the analysis of George Eliot, or the reverent scepticism of Thackeray. And all this works back, I think, to a real thing in him, that he wished to have an obstreperous and incalculable enemy. He wished to keep alive the idea of combat, which means, of necessity, a combat against something individual and alive. I do not know whether, in the kindly rationalism of his epoch, he kept any belief in a personal devil in his theology, but he certainly created a personal devil in every one of his books.

A good example of the meaning can be found, for instance, in such a character as Quilp. Dickens may, for all I know, have had originally some idea of describing Quilp as the bitter and unhappy cripple, a deformity whose mind is stunted along with his body. But if he had such an idea, he soon abandoned it. Quilp is not in the least unhappy. His

whole picturesqueness consists in the fact that he has a kind of hellish
happiness, an atrocious hilarity that makes him go bounding about like
an india-rubber ball. Quilp is not in the least bitter; he has an unaffected
gaiety, an expansiveness, an universality. He desires to hurt people in the
same hearty way that a good-natured man desires to help them. He likes
to poison people with the same kind of clamorous camaraderie with
which an honest man likes to stand their drink. Quilp is not in the least
stunted in mind; he is not in reality even stunted in body—his body, that
is, does not in any way fall short of what he wants it to do. His smallness
gives him rather the promptitude of a bird or the precipitance of a
bullet. In a word, Quilp is precisely the devil of the Middle Ages; he
belongs to that amazingly healthy period when even the lost spirits were
hilarious.

   This heartiness and vivacity in the villains of Dickens is worthy of
note because it is directly connected with his own cheerfulness. This is
a truth little understood in our time, but it is a very essential one. If
optimism means a general approval, it is certainly true that the more a
man becomes an optimist the more he becomes a melancholy man. If he
manages to praise everything, his praise will develop an alarming
resemblance to a polite boredom. He will say that the marsh is as good
as the garden; he will mean that the garden is as dull as the marsh. He
may force himself to say that emptiness is good, but he will hardly
prevent himself from asking what is the good of such good. This
optimism does exist—this optimism which is more hopeless than
pessimism—this optimism which is the very heart of hell. Against such
an aching vacuum of joyless approval there is only one antidote—a
sudden and pugnacious belief in positive evil. This world can be made
beautiful again by beholding it as a battlefield. When we have defined
and isolated the evil thing, the colours come back into everything else.
When evil things have become evil, good things, in a blazing apocalypse,
become good. There are some men who are dreary because they do not
believe in God; but there are many others who are dreary because they
do not believe in the devil. The grass grows green again when we believe
in the devil, the roses grow red again when we believe in the devil.

   No man was more filled with the sense of this bellicose basis of all
cheerfulness than Dickens. He knew very well the essential truth, that
the true optimist can only continue an optimist so long as he is
discontented. For the full value of this life can only be got by fighting;
the violent take it by storm. And if we have accepted everything, we have

missed something—war. This life of ours is a very enjoyable fight, but a very miserable truce. And it appears strange to me that so few critics of Dickens or of other romantic writers have noticed this philosophical meaning in the undiluted villain. The villain is not in the story to be a character; he is there to be a danger—a ceaseless, ruthless, and uncompromising menace, like that of wild beasts or the sea. For the full satisfaction of the sense of combat, which everywhere and always involves a sense of equality, it is necessary to make the evil thing a man; but it is not always necessary, it is not even always artistic, to make him a mixed and probable man. In any tale, the tone of which is at all symbolic, he may quite legitimately be made an aboriginal and infernal energy. It must be a man only in the sense that he must have a wit and will to be matched with the wit and will of the man chiefly fighting. The evil may he human, but it must not be impersonal, which is almost exactly the position occupied by Satan in the theological scheme.

But when all is said, as I have remarked before, the chief fountain in Dickens of what I have called cheerfulness, and some prefer to call optimism, is something deeper than a verbal philosophy. It is, after all, an incomparable hunger and pleasure for the vitality and the variety, for the infinite eccentricity of existence. And this word "eccentricity" brings us, perhaps, nearer to the matter than any other. It is, perhaps, the strongest mark of the divinity of man that he talks of this world as "a strange world," though he has seen no other. We feel that all there is is eccentric, though we do not know what is the centre. This sentiment of the grotesqueness of the universe ran through Dickens' brain and body like the mad blood of the elves. He saw all his streets in fantastic perspectives, he saw all his cockney villas as top heavy and wild, he saw every man's nose twice as big as it was, and every man's eyes like saucers. And this was the basis of his gaiety—the only real basis of any philosophical gaiety. This world is not to be justified as it is justified by the mechanical optimists; it is not to be justified as the best of all possible worlds. Its merit is not that it is orderly and explicable; its merit is that it is wild and utterly unexplained. Its merit is precisely that none of us could have conceived such a thing, that we should have rejected the bare idea of it as miracle and unreason. It is the best of all impossible worlds.

GEORGE GISSING

Characterization

The familiar objection to Dickens's characters, that they are "so unreal" (a criticism common in the mouths of persons who would be the last to tolerate downright verity in fiction), is in part explained—in part justified—by the dramatic conduct of his stories. What unreality there is, arises for the most part from necessities of "plot." This may be illustrated by a comparison between two figures wherein the master has embodied so much homely sweetness and rectitude that both are popular favourites. The boatman Peggotty and Joe Gargery the blacksmith are drawn on similar lines; in both the gentlest nature is manifest beneath a ruggedness proper to their callings. There is a certain resemblance, too, between the stories in which each plays his part; childlike in their simple virtues, both become strongly attached to a child—not their own—living under the same roof, and both suffer a grave disappointment in this affection; the boatman's niece is beguiled from him to her ruin, the blacksmith's little relative grows into a conceited youth ashamed of the old companion and the old home. To readers in general I presume that Peggotty is better known than Joe; *David Copperfield* being more frequently read than *Great Expectations*; but if we compare the two figures as to their "reality," we must decide in favour of Gargery, I think him a better piece of workmanship all round; the prime reason, however, for his standing out so much more solidly in one's mind than Little

From *Charles Dickens*, pp. 96–127. © 1924 by Dodd, Mead, and Co. Reprinted by permission.

Emily's uncle is that he lives in a world, not of melodrama, but of everyday cause and effect. The convict Magwitch and his strange doings make no such demand upon one's credulity as the story of Emily and Steerforth, told as it is, with its extravagant situations and flagrantly artificial development. Pip is so thoroughly alive that we can forget his dim relations with Satis House. But who can put faith in Mr. Peggotty, when he sets forth to search for his niece over the highways and by-ways of Europe? Who can for a moment put faith in Emily herself after she has ceased to be the betrothed of Ham? As easily could one believe that David Copperfield actually overheard that wildly fantastic dialogue in the lodging-house between the lost girl and Rosa Dartle.

Many such examples might be adduced of excellent, or masterly, characterization spoilt by the demand for effective intrigue. We call to mind this or that person in circumstances impossible of credit; and hastily declare that character and situation are alike unreal. And hereby hangs another point worth touching upon, I have heard it very truly remarked that, in our day, people for the most part criticise Dickens from a recollection of their reading in childhood; they do not come fresh to him with mature minds; in general, they never read him at all after childish years. This is an obvious source of much injustice. Dickens is good reading for all times of life, as are all the great imaginative writers. Let him be read by children together with Don Quixote. But who can speak with authority of Cervantes who knows him only from an acquaintance made at ten years old? To the mind of a child Dickens is, or ought to be, fascinating—(alas for the whole subject of children's reading nowadays!)—and most of the fascination is due to that romantic treatment of common life which is part, indeed, of Dickens's merit, but has smaller value and interest to the older mind. Much of his finest humour is lost upon children; much of his perfect description, and all his highest achievement in characterization. Taking Dickens "as read," people inflict a loss upon themselves and do a wrong to the author. Who, in childhood, ever cared much for *Little Dorrit*? The reason is plain; in this book Dickens has comparatively little of his wonted buoyancy; throughout, it is in a graver key. True, a house falls down in a most exciting way, and this the reader will remember; all else is to him a waste. We hear, accordingly, that nothing good can be said for *Little Dorrit*. Whereas, a competent judge, taking up the book as he would any other, will find in it some of the best work Dickens ever did; and especially in this matter of characterization; pictures so wholly admirable, so marvellously observed and so exquisitely presented, that he is tempted to place *Little Dorrit* among the best of the novels.

Again, it is not unusual to seek in Dickens's characters for something he never intended to be there; in other words, his figures are often slighted because they represent a class in society which lacks many qualities desired by cultivated readers, and possesses very prominently the distasteful features such a critic could well dispense with. You lay down, for instance, Thackeray's *Pendennis*, and soon after you happen to take up *Dombey and Son*. Comparisons arise. Whilst reading of Major Bagstock, you find your thoughts wandering to Major Pendennis; when occupied (rather disdainfully) with Mr. Toots, you suddenly recall Foker. What can be the immediate outcome of such contrast? It seems impossible to deny to Thackeray a great superiority in the drawing of character; his aristocratic Major and his wealthy young jackass are so much more "real," that is to say, so much more familiar, than the promoted vulgarian Bagstock and the enriched whipper-snapper Toots. A hasty person would be capable of exclaiming that Dickens had plainly taken suggestions from Thackeray, and made but poor use of them. Observe, however, that *Dombey and Son* appeared, complete, in 1848; *Pendennis* in 1849. Observe, too, the explanation of the whole matter: that Bagstock and Toots represent quite as truthfully figures possible in a certain class, as do Thackeray's characters those to be found in a rank distinctly higher. If Thackeray (who needed no suggestions from others' books) was indeed conscious of this whimsical parallel, we can only admire the skill and finish with which he worked it out. But assuredly he dreamt of no slight to Dickens's performance. They had wrought in different material. Social distinctions are sufficiently pronounced even in our time of revolution; fifty years ago they were much more so. And precisely what estranges the cultivated reader in Bagstock and Toots, is nothing more nor less than evidence of their creator's truthfulness.

A wider question confronts one in looking steadfastly at the masterpieces of a novelist concerned with the lower, sometimes the lowest, modes of life in a great city. Among all the names immortalized by Dickens none is more widely familiar than that of Mrs. Gamp. It is universally admitted that in Mrs. Gamp we have a creation such as can be met with only in the greatest writers; a figure at once individual and typical; a marvel of humorous presentment; vital in the highest degree attainable by this art of fiction. From the day of her first appearance on the stage, Mrs. Gamp has been a delight, a wonder, a by-word. She stands unique, no other novelist can show a piece of work, in the same kind, worthy of a place beside her; we must go to the very heights of world-literature, to him who bodied forth Dame Quickly, and Juliet's nurse, for the suggestion of equivalent power. Granted, then, that Mrs. Gamp has indubitable existence; who and what is she? Well, a so-called nurse, living in Kingsgate Street, Holborn, in a filthy room somewhere upstairs, and summoned for nursing of all kinds by persons more or less well-to-do, who are so unfortunate as to know of no less offensive substitute. We are told, and can believe, that in the year 1844 (the date of *Martin Chuzzlewit*) few people did know of any substitute for Mrs. Gamp; that she was an institution; that she carried her odious vices and her criminal incompetence from house to house in decent parts of London. Dickens knew her only too well; had observed her at moments of domestic crisis; had learnt her language and could reproduce it (or most of it) with surprising accuracy. In plain words, then, we are speaking of a very loathsome creature; a sluttish, drunken, avaricious, dishonest woman. Meeting her in the flesh, we should shrink disgusted, so well does the foulness of her person correspond with the baseness of her mind. Hearing her speak, we should turn away in half-amused contempt. Yet, when we encounter her in the pages of Dickens, we cannot have too much of Mrs. Gamp's company; her talk is an occasion of uproarious mirth; we never dream of calling her to moral judgment, but laugh the more, the more infamously she sees fit to behave. Now, in what sense can this figure in literature be called a copy of the human original?

I am perfectly aware that this inquiry goes to the roots of the theory of Art. Here I have no space (nor would it be the proper moment) to discuss all the issues that are involved in a question so direct and natural; but if we are to talk at all about the people in Dickens, we must needs start with some understanding of what is implied when we call them true, lifelike, finely presented. Is not the fact in itself very remarkable, that by dint (it seems) of *omitting* those very features which in life most strongly impress us, an artist in fiction can produce something which we applaud as an inimitable portrait? That for disgust he can give us delight, and yet leave us glorying in his verisimilitude?

Turn to another art. Open the great volume of Hogarth, and look at the several figures of women which present a fair correspondence with that of Mrs. Gamp. We admire the artist's observation, his great skill, his moral significance, even his grim humour; then—we close the book with a feeling of relief. With these faces who would spend hours of leisure? The thing has been supremely well done, and we are glad of it, and will praise the artist unreservedly; but his basely grinning and leering women must not hang upon the wall, to be looked at and talked of with all and sundry. Hogarth has copied—in the strict sense of the word. He gives us life—and we cannot bear it.

The Mrs. Gamp of our novel is a piece of the most delicate idealism. It is a sublimation of the essence of Gamp. No novelist (say what he will) ever gave us a picture of life which was not idealized; but there are degrees—degrees of purpose and of power. Juliet's Nurse is an idealized portrait, but it comes much nearer to the real thing than Mrs. Gamp; in our middle-class England we cannot altogether away with the free-spoken dame of Verona; we Bowdlerize her—of course damaging her in the process. Mrs. Berry, in *Richard Feverel*, is idealized, but she smacks too strongly of the truth for boudoir readers. Why, Moll Flanders herself is touched and softened, for all the author's illusive directness. In Mrs. Gamp, Dickens has done his own Bowdlerizing, but with a dexterity which serves only to heighten his figure's effectiveness. Vulgarity he leaves; that is of the essence of the matter; vulgarity unsurpassable is the note of Mrs. Gamp. Vileness, on the other hand, becomes grotesquerie, wonderfully converted into a subject of laughter. Her speech, among the basest ever heard from human tongue, by a process of infinite subtlety, which leaves it the same yet not the same, is made an endless amusement, a source of quotation for laughing lips incapable of unclean utterance.

Idealism, then: confessed idealism. But let us take another character from another book, also a woman supposed to represent a phase of low life in London. Do you recall "good Mrs. Brown," the hag who strips little Florence Dombey of her clothes? And do you remember that this creature has a daughter, her name Alice Marlow, who—presumably having been a domestic servant, or a shop-girl, or something of the kind—was led astray by Mr. Carker of the shining teeth, and has become a wandering nondescript? Now in Alice Marlow we again have idealism; but of a different kind. This child of good Mrs. Brown, tramping into London on a bitter night, is found on the roadside and charitably taken home by Mr. Carker's sister, neither being aware of the other's identity; and having submitted to this kindness, and having accepted money, the girl goes her way. That same night she learns who has befriended her, and forthwith rushes back (a few miles) through storm and darkness, to fling the alms at the giver. Outlines of a story sufficiently theatrical; but the dialogue! One fails to understand how Dickens brought himself to pen the language which—at great length— he puts into this puppet's mouth. It is doubtful whether one could pick out a single sentence, a single phrase, such as the real Alice Marlow could conceivably have used. Her passion is vehement; no impossible thing. The words in which she utters it would be appropriate to the most stagey of wronged heroines—be that who it may. A figure less lifelike will not be found in any novel ever written. Yet Dickens doubtless intended it as legitimate idealization; a sort of type of the doleful multitude of betrayed women. He meant it for imagination exalting common fact. But the fact is not exalted; it has simply vanished. And the imagination is of a kind that avails nothing on any theme. In Mrs. Gamp a portion of truth is omitted; in Alice Marlow there is substitution of falsity. By the former process, true idealism *may* be reached; by the latter, one arrives at nothing but attitude and sham.

Of course omission and veiling do not suffice to create Mrs. Gamp. In his alchemy, Dickens had command of the *menstruum* which alone is powerful enough to effect such transmutation as this; it is called humour. Humour, be it remembered, is inseparable from charity. Not only did it enable him to see this coarse creature as an amusing person; it inspired him with that large tolerance which looks through things external, gives its full weight to circumstance, and preserves a modesty, a humility, in human judgment. We can form some notion of what Mrs. Gamp would have become in the hands of a rigorous realist, with scorn and disgust (inevitably implied) taking the place of humour. We reject the photograph; it avails us nothing in art or life. Humour deals gently with fact and fate; in its smile there is forbearance, in its laugh there is kindliness. With falsehood—however well meant—it is incompatible; when it has done its work as solvent, the gross adherents are dissipated, the essential truth remains. Do you ask for the Platonic *idea* of London's hired nurse early in Queen Victoria's reign? Dickens shows it you embodied. At such a thing as this, crawling between earth and heaven, what can one do but laugh? Its existence is a puzzle, a wonder. The class it represents shall be got rid of as speedily as possible; well and good; we cannot tolerate such a public nuisance. But the type shall be preserved for all time by the magic of a great writer's deep-seeing humour, and shall be known as Mrs. Gamp.

For a moment, contrast with this masterpiece a picture in which Dickens has used his idealism on material more promising, though sought amid surroundings sufficiently like those seen in the description of Kingsgate Street. The most successful character in his stories written to be read at Christmas is Mrs. Lirriper. She belongs to a class distinguished then, as now, by its uncleanness, its rapacity, its knavery, its ignorance. Mrs. Lirriper keeps a London lodging-house. Here, in depicting an individual, Dickens has not typified a class. He idealizes this woman, but finds in her, ready to his hand, the qualities of goodness and tenderness and cheery honesty, so that there is no question of transmuting a subject repulsive to the senses. Mrs. Lirriper is quite possible, even in a London lodging-house; in the flesh, however, we should not exactly seek her society. Her talk (idealized with excellent adroitness) would too often jar upon the ear; her person would be, to say the least, unattractive. In the book, she has lost these accidents of position: we are first amused, then drawn on to like, to admire, to love her. An unfortunate blemish—the ever-recurring artificiality of story—threatens to make her dim; but Mrs. Lirriper triumphs over this. We bear her in memory as a person known—a person most unhappily circumstanced, set in a gloomy sphere; but of such sweet nature that we forget her inevitable defects, even as we should those of an actual acquaintance of like character.

In looking back on the events of life, do we not see them otherwise than, at the time, they appeared to us? The harsh is smoothed; the worst of everything is forgotten; things pleasant come into relief. This (a great argument for optimism) is a similitude of Dickens's art. Like Time, he obscures the unpleasing, emphasizes all we are glad to remember. Time does not falsify; neither does Dickens, whenever his art is unalloyed.

Let us turn to his literary method. It is that of all the great novelists. To set before his reader the image so vivid in his own mind, he simply describes and reports. We have, in general, a very precise and complete picture of externals—the face, the gesture, the habit. In this Dickens excels; he proves to us by sheer force of visible detail how distinct was the mental shape from which he drew. We learn the tone of voice, the trick of utterance; he declared that every word spoken by his characters was audible to him. Then does the man reveal himself in colloquy; sometimes once for all, sometimes by degrees, in chapter after chapter—though this is seldom the case. We know these people because we see and hear them.

In a few instances he added deliberate analysis; it was never well done, always superfluous. Very rarely has analysis of character justified itself in fiction. To Dickens the method was alien; he could make no use whatever of it. In the early book which illustrates all his defects, *Nicholas Nickleby*, we have some dreary pages concerned with the inner man of Ralph Nickleby; seeing that the outer is but shadowy, these details cannot interest; they show, moreover, much crudity and conventionality of thought. Later, an analysis is attempted of Mr. Dombey—very laborious, very long. It does not help us in the least to understand Paul's father, himself one of the least satisfactory of Dickens's leading persons. One may surmise that the author felt something of this, and went out of his wonted way in an endeavour to give the image more life.

It results from Dickens's weakness in the devising of incident, in the planning of story, that he seldom develops character through circumstance. There are conversions, but we do not much believe in them; they smack of the stage. Possibly young Martin Chuzzlewit may be counted an exception; but there is never much life in him. From this point of view Dickens's best bit of work is Pip, in *Great Expectations*: Pip, the narrator of his own story, who exhibits very well indeed the growth of a personality, the interaction of character and event. One is not permitted to lose sight of the actual author; though so much more living than Esther Summerson, Pip is yet embarrassed, like her, with the gift of humour. We know very well whose voice comes from behind the scenes when Pip is describing Mr. Wopsle's dramatic venture. Save for this, we acknowledge a true self-revelation. What could be better than a lad's picture of his state of mind, when, after learning that he has "great expectations," he quits the country home of his childhood and goes to London? "I formed a plan in outline for bestowing a dinner of roast beef and plum-pudding, a pint of ale, and a gallon of condescension upon everybody in the village" (chap. xix). It is one of many touches which give high value to this book.

As a rule, the more elaborate Dickens's conception of character, the smaller his success in working it out. Again and again he endeavoured to present men and women of exceptionally strong passions: the kind of persons who make such a figure on the boards, where they frown and clench their fists, and utter terrible phrases. It began in *Oliver Twist* with the man called Monk; in *Barnaby* came the murderer; in *Chuzzlewit* appears the puppet known as old Martin, a thing of sawdust. Later, the efforts in this direction are more conscientious, more laboured, but rarely more successful. An exception, perhaps, may be noted in Bradley Headstone, the lover of Lizzie Hexam, whose consuming passion here and there convinces, all the more for its well-contrived contrast with the character of the man whom Lizzie prefers. Charley Hexam, too, is lifelike, on a lower plane. The popular voice pleads for Sydney Carton; yes, he is well presented—but so easy to forget. Think, on the other hand, of the long list of women meant to be tragic, who, one and all, must be judged failures. Edith Dombey, with her silent wrath and ludicrous behaviour, who, intended for a strong, scornful nature, dumbly goes to the sacrifice when bidden by her foolish mother, and then rails at the old worldling for the miseries needlessly brought upon herself. Rosa Dartle, at first a promising suggestion, but falling away into exaggerations of limelight frenzy. Lady Dedlock and her maid Hortense—which is the more obvious waxwork? Mrs. Clennam, in *Little Dorrit*, is wrought so patiently and placed in so picturesque a scene that one laments over her impossibility; her so-called talk is, perhaps, less readable than anything in Dickens. The same book shows us, or aims at showing us, Miss Wade and Tattycoram, from both of whom we turn incredulous. Of Miss Havisham one grudges to speak; her ghostly presence does its best to spoil an admirable novel. Women, all these, only in name; a cause of grief to the lovers of the master, a matter of scoffing to his idler critics. When we come to women of everyday stature, then indeed it is a different thing. So numerous are these, and so important in an estimate of Dickens's power of characterization, that I must give them a chapter to themselves.

Neither at a black-hearted villain was he really good, though he prided himself on his achievements in this kind. Jonas Chuzzlewit is the earliest worth mention; and what can be said of Jonas, save that he is a surly ruffian of whom one knows very little? The "setting" of his part is very strong; much powerful writing goes to narrate his history; but the man remains mechanical. Mr. Carker hardly aims at such completeness of scoundreldom, but he would be a fierce rascal—if not so bent on exhibiting his teeth, which remind one of the working wires. Other shapes hover in lurid vagueness. Whether, last of all, John Jasper would have shown a great advance, must remain doubtful. The first half of *Edwin Drood* shows him picturesquely, and little more. We discover no hint of real tragedy. The man seems to us a very vulgar assassin, and we care not at all what becomes of him.

Against these set the gallery of portraits in which Dickens has
displayed to us the legal world of his day. Here he painted from nature,
and with an artist's love of his subject. From the attorneys and barristers
of *Pickwick*, sportive themselves and a cause of infinite mirth in others,
to the Old Bailey practitioners so admirably grim in *Great Expectations*,
one's eye passes along a row of masterpieces. Nay, it is idle to use the
pictorial simile; here are men with blood in their veins—some of them
with a good deal of it on their hands. They will not be forgotten;
whether we watch the light comedy of Jorkins and Spenlow, or observe
the grim gravity of Mr. Jaggers, it is with the same entire conviction. In
this department of his work Dickens can be said to idealize only in the
sense of the finest art; no praise can exaggerate his dexterity in setting
forth these examples of supreme realism. As a picture of actual life in a
certain small world *Bleak House* is his greatest book; from office-boy to
judge, here are all who walk in "the valley of the shadow of the Law."
Impossible to run through the list, much as one would enjoy it. Think
only of Mr. Vholes. In the whole range of fiction there is no character
more vivid than this; exhibited so briefly yet so completely, with such
rightness in every touch, such impressiveness of total effect, that the
thing becomes a miracle. No strain of improbable intrigue can threaten
the vitality of these dusty figures. The clerks are as much alive, as their
employers; the law-stationer stands for ever face to face with Mr.
Tulkinghorn; Inspector Bucket has warmer flesh than that of any other
detective in the library of detective literature. As for Jaggers and
Wemmick, we should presume them unsurpassable had we not known
their predecessors. They would make a novelist's reputation.

Among the finest examples of characterization (I postpone a review
of the figures which belong more distinctly to satire) must be mentioned
the Father of the Marshalsea. Should ever proof be demanded—as often
it has been—that Dickens is capable of high comedy, let it be sought in
the 31st chapter of book i of *Little Dorrit*. There will be seen the old
Marshalsea prisoner, the bankrupt of half a lifetime, entertaining and
patronizing his workhouse pensioner, old Mr. Nandy. For delicacy of
treatment, for fineness of observation, this scene, I am inclined to think,
is unequalled in all the novels. Of exaggeration there is no trace; nothing
raises a laugh; at most one smiles, and may very likely be kept grave by
profound interest and a certain emotion of wonder. We are in a debtors'
prison, among vulgar folk; yet the exquisite finish of this study of human
nature forbids one to judge it by any but the highest standards. The

Dorrit brothers are both well drawn; they are characterizations in the best sense of the word; and in this scene we have the culmination of the author's genius. That it reveals itself so quietly is but the final assurance of consummate power.

With the normal in character, with what (all things considered) we may call wholesome normality, Dickens does not often concern himself. Of course there are his homely-minded "little women," of whom more in another place. And there are his benevolent old boys (I call them so advisedly) whom one would like to be able to class with everyday people, but who cannot in strictness be considered here. Walking-gentlemen appear often enough; amiable shadows, such as Tom Pinch's friend Westlock; figures meant to be prominent, such as Arthur Clennam. There remain a few instances of genuine characterization within ordinary limits. I cannot fall in with the common judgment that Dickens never shows us a gentleman. Twice, certainly, he has done so, with the interesting distinction that in one case he depicts a gentleman of the old school; in the other, a representative of the refined manhood which came into existence (or became commonly observable) in his latter years. In John Jarndyce I can detect no vulgarity; he appears to me compact of good sense, honour, and gentle feeling. His eccentricity does not pass bounds; the better we know him the less observable it grows. Though we are told nothing expressly of his intellectual acquirements, it is plain that he had a liberal education, and that his tastes are studious. Impossible not to like and to respect Mr. Jarndyce. Compare him with Mr. Pickwick, or with the Cheerybles, and we see at once the author's indication of social superiority, no less than his increased skill in portraiture. The second figure, belonging to a changed time, is Mr. Crisparkle, for whose sake especially one regrets the unfinished state of *Edwin Drood*. His breezy manner, his athletic habits, his pleasant speech, give no bad idea of the classical tutor who is neither an upstart nor a pedant. Dickens was careful in his choice of names; we see how he formed that of Crisparkle, and recognize its fitness.

Two other names occur to me, which carry with them a suggestion of true gentility—if the word be permitted; but their bearers can hardly rank with normal personages. Sir Leicester Dedlock, though by no means unsympathetically presented, belongs rather to the region of satire; he is a gentleman, indeed, and meant to be representative of a class, but his special characteristic overcharges the portrait. Incomparably more of a human being than his wife, he might, with less satirical emphasis, have been a very true gentleman indeed. Then, in *Dombey and Son*, does one not remember Cousin Feenix? The name, this time, is unfortunate; this weak-legged scion of aristocracy deserved better treatment. For he is no phantasm; has no part with the puppets of supposed high-birth whom Dickens occasionally set up only for the pleasure of knocking them down again. However incapable of walking straight across a room, however restricted in his views of life, Cousin Feenix has the instincts of birth and breeding. I think one may say that he is Dickens's least disputable success in a sketch (it is only a sketch) from the aristocratic world. His talk does not seem to me exaggerated, and it is unusually interesting; his heart is right, his apprehensions are delicate. That he should be shown as feeble in mind, no less than at the knees, is merely part of the author's scheme; and, after all, the feebleness is more apparent than real. Dickens, moreover, very often associates kindness of disposition with lack of brains; it connects itself, I fancy, with his attitude towards liberal education, which has already been discussed, as well as with his Radicalism, still to be spoken of. No distinctly intellectual person figures in his books; David Copperfield is only a seeming exception, for who really thinks of David as a literary man? To his autobiography let all praise be given—with the reserve that we see the man himself less clearly than any other person of whom he speaks. Decidedly he is *not* "the hero of his own story." Had Dickens intended to show us a man of letters, he would here have failed most grievously; of course he aimed at no such thing; the attempt would have cost him half his public. And so it is that one never thinks of the good David as a character at all, never for a moment credits *him*, the long-suffering youth for whom Dora "held the pens," with that glorious endowment of genius which went to the writing of his life.

Of an average middle-class family in Dickens's earlier time—decent, kindly, not unintelligent folk—we have the best example in the Meagles group, from *Little Dorrit*. This household may be contrasted with, say, that of the Maylies in *Oliver Twist*, which is merely immature work, and with the more familiar family circles on which Dickens lavishes his mirth and his benevolence. The Meagles do not much interest us, which is quite right; they are thoroughly realized, and take their place in social history. Well done, too, is the Pocket family in *Great Expectations*, an interesting pendant to that of the Jellybys in *Bleak House*; showing how well, when he chose, Dickens could satirize without extravagance. Mrs. Pocket is decidedly more credible than Mrs. Jellyby;

it might be urged, perhaps, that she belongs to the Sixties instead of to the Fifties, a point of some importance. The likeness in dissimilitude between these ladies' husbands is very instructive. As for the son, Herbert Pocket, he is a capital specimen of the healthy, right-minded, and fairly-educated middle-class youth. Very skilfully indeed is he placed side by side with Pip; each throwing into relief the other's natural and acquired characteristics. We see how long it will take the blacksmith's foster-child (he telling the tale himself) to reach the point of mental and moral refinement to which Herbert Pocket has been bred.

One more illustration of the ordinary in life and character. Evidently Dickens took much pains with Walter Gay, in *Dombey and Son*, meaning to represent an average middle-class boy, high-spirited, frank, affectionate, and full of cheerful ambition. I have already mentioned the darker design, so quickly abandoned; we feel sure its working out would not have carried conviction, for Walter Gay, from the first, does not ring quite true. The note seems forced; we are not stirred by the lad's exuberance of jollity, and he never for a moment awakens strong interest. Is it any better with Richard Carstone,—in whom the tragic idea was, with modification, carried through? Yes, Richard is more interesting; by necessity of his fortunes, and by virtue of artistic effort. He has his place in a book pervaded with the atmosphere of doom. Vivid he never becomes; we see him as a passive victim of fate, rather than as a struggling man; if he made a better fight, or if we were allowed to see more of his human weakness (partly forbidden by our proprieties), his destiny would affect us more than it does. In truth, this kind of thing cannot be done under Dickens's restrictions. Thackeray *could* have done it magnificently; but there was "the great, big, stupid public."

The "gentleman" Dickens loved to contemplate was—in echo of Burns's phrase—he who derives his patent of gentility straight from Almighty God. These he found abundantly among the humble of estate, the poor in spirit; or indulged his fine humanity in the belief that they abounded. A broken squire, reduced to miserly service, but keeping through all faults and misfortunes the better part of his honest and kindly nature; grotesque in person, of fantastic demeanour, but always lovable;—of this dream comes Newman Noggs. A city clerk, grey in conscientious labour for one house, glorying in the perfection of his ledger, taking it ill if his employers insist on raising his salary;—the vision is christened Tim Linkinwater. A young man of bumpkinish appearance, shy, ungainly, who has somehow drifted into the household of a country architect; who nourishes his soul at the church organ; who is so good and simple and reverential that years of experience cannot teach him what everyone else sees at a glance—the hypocritical rascality of his master: he takes shape, and is known to us as Tom Pinch. A village blacksmith, with heart as tender as his thews are tough; delighting above all things in the society of a little child; so dull of brain that he gives up in despair the effort to learn his alphabet; so sweet of temper that he endures in silence the nagging of an outrageous wife; so delicate of sensibility that he perspires at the thought of seeming to intrude upon an old friend risen in life;—what name can be his but Joe Gargery? These, and many another like unto them, did the master lovingly create, and there would be something of sacrilege in a cold scrutiny of his work. Whether or no their prototypes existed in the hurrying crowd of English life, which obscures so much good as well as evil, these figures have fixed themselves in the English imagination, and their names are part of our language. Dickens saw them, and heard them speak; to us, when we choose to enjoy without criticising, they seem no less present. Every such creation was a good deed; the results for good have been incalculable. Would he have been better occupied, had he pried into each character, revealed its vices, insisted on its sordid weaknesses, thrown bare its frequent hypocrisy, and emphasized its dreary unintelligence? Indeed, I think not. I will only permit myself the regret that he who could come so near to truth, and yet so move the affections, as in Joe Gargery, was at other times content with that inferior idealism which addresses itself only to unripe minds or to transitory moods.

The point to be kept in view regarding these ideal figures is that, however little their speech or conduct may smack of earth, their worldly surroundings are shown with marvellous fidelity. Tom Pinch worshipping at the shrine of Pecksniff may not hold our attention; but Tom Pinch walking towards Salisbury on the frosty road, or going to market in London with his sister, is unforgettable. This is what makes the difference between an impossible person in Dickens and the same kind of vision in the work of smaller writers. One cannot repeat too often that, in our literary slang, he "visualized" every character, Little Nell no less than Mr. Jaggers. Seeing *them*, he saw the house in which they lived, the table at which they ate, and all the little habits of their day-to-day life. Here is an invaluable method of illusion, if an author can adopt it. Thus fortified, Dickens's least substantial imaginings have a durability not to be hoped for the laborious accuracies of an artist uninspired.

Pass to another group in this scarcely exhaustible world—the confessed eccentrics. Here Dickens revels. An English novelist must needs be occupied to some extent with grotesque abnormalities of thought and demeanour. Dickens saw them about him even more commonly than we of to-day, and delighted in noting, selecting, combining. The result is seen in those persons of his drama who are frankly given up by many who will defend his verisimilitude in other directions. Mantalini, for example; Quilp, Captain Cuttle, Silas Wegg, and many another. For Silas Wegg, I fear, nothing can be urged, save the trifle that we know him; he becomes a bore, one of the worst instances of this form of humour weakened by extenuation. Even Dickens occasionally suffered from the necessity of filling a certain space. Think how long his novels are, and marvel that the difficulty does not more often declare itself. Of Mr. Boythorn we are accustomed to think as drawn from Landor, but then it is Landor with all the intellect left out; his roaring as gently as any sucking-dove does not greatly charm us, but his talk has good qualities. More of a character, in the proper sense of the word, is Harold Skimpole, whose portrait gave such offence to Leigh Hunt. Now Skimpole is one of the few people in Dickens whom we dislike, and so, *a priori*, demands attention. If we incline to think his eccentricity overdone, be it remembered that the man was in part an actor, and a very clever actor too. Skimpole is excellent work, and stands out with fine individuality in contrast to the representatives of true unworldliness.

To which category belongs Mr. Micawber? The art of living without an income may be successfully cultivated in very different moods. It is possible for a man of the most generous instincts to achieve great things in this line of endeavour; but the fact remains that, sooner or later, somebody has the honour of discharging his liabilities. To speak severely of Mr. Micawber is beyond the power of the most conscientious critic, whether in life or art; the most rigid economist would be glad to grasp him by the hand and to pay for the bowl of punch over which this type of genial impecuniosity would dilate upon his embarrassments and his hopes; the least compromising realist has but to open at a dialogue or a letter in which Mr. Micawber's name is seen, and straightway he forgets his theories. No selfish intention can be attributed to him. His bill might *not* be provided for when he declared it *was*, and, in consequence, poor Traddles may lose the table he has purchased for "the dearest girl in the world," but Mr. Micawber had all the time been firmly assured that something would turn up; he will sympathize profoundly with Traddles, and write him an epistle which makes amends for the loss of many tables. No man ever lived who was so consistently delightful—certainly Dickens's father cannot have been so, but in this idealized portraiture we have essential truth. Men of this stamp do not abound, but they are met with, even today. As a rule, he who waits for something to turn up, mixing punch the while, does so with a very keen eye on his neighbour's pocket, and is recommended to us neither by Skimpole's fantastic gaiety nor by Micawber's eloquence and warmth of heart; nevertheless, one knows the irrepressibly hopeful man, full of kindliness, often distinguished by unconscious affectations of speech, who goes through life an unreluctant pensioner on the friends won by his many good and genial qualities. The one point on which experience gives no support to the imaginative figure is his conversion to practical activity. Mr. Micawber in Australia does the heart good; but he is a pious vision. We refuse to think of a wife worn out by anxieties, of children growing up in squalor; we gladly accept the flourishing colonist; but this is tribute to the author whom we love. Dickens never wrought more successfully for our pleasure and for his own fame. He is ever at his best when dealing with an amiable weakness. And in Micawber he gives us no purely national type; such men are peculiar to no country; all the characteristics of this wonderful picture can be appreciated by civilized readers throughout the world. It is not so in regard to many of his creations, though all the finest have traits of universal humanity. Should time deal hardly with him, should his emphasis of time and place begin to weigh against his wide acceptance, it is difficult to believe that the beaming visage of Wilkins Micawber will not continue to be recognized wherever men care for literary art.

This chapter must conclude with a glance at a class of human beings prominent in Dickens's earlier books, but of small artistic interest when treated in the manner peculiar to him. He was fond of characters hovering between eccentricity and madness, and in one case he depicted what he himself calls an idiot, though idiocy is not strictly speaking the form of disease exhibited. Lunatics were more often found at large in his day than in ours; perhaps that accounts for our introduction to such persons as Mrs. Nickleby's wooer and Mr. Dick; Miss Flite, of course, had another significance. The crazy gentleman on the garden walk, who at once flatters and terrifies Mrs. Nickleby, can hardly be regarded as anything but an actor in broad farce; his talk, indeed, is midsummer madness, but is meant only to raise a laugh. In the new century, one does not laugh with such agreeable facility. Mrs. Nickleby commands our attention—at a respectful distance; and here, as always, behaves after her kind, illustrating the eternal feminine; but the madman we cannot accept. Betsy Trotwood's *protégé* comes nearer to the recognizable; nevertheless Mr. Dick's presence in such a book as *David Copperfield* would seem waste of space, but for certain considerations. He illustrates the formidable lady's goodness and common-sense; he served a very practical purpose, that of recommending rational treatment of the insane; and he had his place in the pages of an author whose humanity includes all that are in any way afflicted, in mind, body, or estate. Moreover, the craze about King Charles's head has been, and is likely to be, a great resource to literary persons in search of a familiar allusion. In passing to *Barnaby Rudge*, we are on different ground. Whatever else, Barnaby is a very picturesque figure, and I presume it was merely on this account that Dickens selected such a hero. In an earlier chapter, I said that this story seemed to me to bear traces of the influence of Scott; its narrative style and certain dialogues in the historical part are suggestive of this. May not the crazy Barnaby have originated in a recollection of Madge Wildfire? Crazy, I call him; an idiot he certainly is not. An idiot does not live a life of exalted imagination. But certain lunatics are of imagination all compact, and Barnaby, poetically speaking, makes a good representative of the class. Of psychology—a word unknown to Dickens—we, of course, have nothing; to ask for it is out of place. The idea, all things considered, cannot be judged a happy one. Whilst writing the latter part of the book Dickens thought for a moment of showing the rioters as led by a commanding figure, who, in the end, should prove to have escaped from Bedlam. We see his motive for this, but are not sorry he abandoned the idea. Probably *Barnaby Rudge*, good as it is, would have been still better had the suggestion of a half-witted central figure been also discarded.

Chronology

1812	Born Charles John Huffam Dickens on February 7 in Portsmouth, England.
1814	Dickens family relocates to London.
1816	Charles' first official schooling.
1821	Financial disaster; Dickens family relocates to Chatham.
1822	Relocation to Camden Town.
1824	John Dickens imprisoned in the Marshalsea; Charles begins work at Warren's Blacking Factory; John Dickens released in May.
1827	Removed from school; works in attorney's office.
1829	Employed as freelance reporter.
1830	Meets Maria Beadnell.
1833	Is jilted by Beadnell; first published story appears ("Dinner at Poplar Walk," *Monthly Magazine*).
1834	Becomes "Boz"; meets Catherine Hogarth.
1835	Becomes engaged to Catherine Hogarth.
1836	Is married to Catherine Hogarth on April 2; first Boz sketches appear; edits *Bentley's Miscellany*; is introduced to Forster; *Pickwick* begins.
1837	First child born in January; Mary Hogarth, living with the Dickenses, dies in Charles' arms; Dickens begins *Oliver Twist*.

1838	Begins *Nicholas Nickleby*.
1839	Leaves the *Miscellany*.
1840	*Master Humphrey's Clock* introduced; begins *The Old Curiosity Shop*.
1840–41	*The Old Curiosity Shop* appears in *Master Humphrey's Clock*.
1841	*Barnaby Rudge* appears in *Master Humphrey's Clock*; travels with Catherine to Scotland.
1842	Visits the United States and Canada with Catherine and is lavishly received; produces *American Notes*, which is found offensive; Georgina Hogarth resides with Dickenses.
1843	*A Christmas Carol*; begins *Martin Chuzzlewit*.
1844	Journeys to Italy and, later, returns to Genoa; *The Chimes*.
1845	Begins amateur theatrical company; *The Cricket and the Hearth*.
1846	Journeys to Switzerland and France; begins *Dombey and Son*; *The Battle of Life*.
1848	Tries hand at autobiography; *The Haunted Man*.
1849–50	*David Copperfield*.
1850	Founds *Household Words*.
1851–53	*Bleak House*.
1853	Begins public readings of his work.
1854	*Hard Times*.
1855	Reunited, disastrously, with Maria Beadnell (Mrs. Henry Winter); *Little Dorrit* begins.
1856	Collaborates with Collins on *The Frozen Deep*; purchases Gad's Hill Place.
1857	Meets Ellen (Nellie) Ternan while co-starring with her and her mother in his and Collins' *The Frozen Deep*; Dickens and Catherine take separate bedrooms.
1858	Catherine accuses him of having an affair (in the spring); separated from Catherine; quells rumors about relationship with Georgina Hogarth; begins paid readings of his work.

1859	*A Tale of Two Cities.*
1860	Family relocates to Gad's Hill; *Great Expectations.*
1864	Health begins to fail from strain of work and public readings; *Our Mutual Friend.*
1865	Train from Paris derails on a bridge, endangering Dickens and Ellen Ternan; Dickens rescues the manuscript of *Our Mutual Friend.*
1867–68	Visits United States again.
1869	*The Mystery of Edwin Drood.*
1870	Final public readings; dies of paralytic stroke; is buried in Westminster Abbey.

Works by Charles Dickens

Sketches by "Boz," Illustrative of Every-day Life and Every-day People. 1836.

Sunday under Three Heads. 1836.

The Village Coquettes: A Comic Opera. 1836.

The Posthumous Papers of the Pickwick Club. 1836–37.

The Strange Gentleman: A Comic Burletta. 1837.

Memoirs of Joseph Grimaldi (editor). 1838.

Sketches of Young Gentlemen. 1838.

Oliver Twist; or, The Parish Boy's Progress. 1838.

The Life and Adventures of Nicholas Nickleby. 1838–39.

The Loving Ballad of Lord Bateman (with William Makepeace Thackeray). 1839.

Sketches of Young Couples. 1840.

Master Humphrey's Clock; The Old Curiosity Shop; Barnaby Rudge. 1840–41.

The Pic Nic Papers (editor). 1841.

American Notes. 1842.

A Christmas Carol in Prose: Being a Ghost-Story of Christmas. 1843.

The Life and Adventures of Martin Chuzzlewit, His Relatives, Friends and Enemies. 1843–44.

The Chimes: A Goblin Story of Some Bells That Rang an Old Year Out and a New Year In. 1845.

The Cricket on the Hearth: A Fairy Tale of Home. 1846.

Pictures from Italy. 1846.

The Battle of Life: A Love Story. 1846.

Dealings with the Firm of Dombey and Son Wholesale, Retail and for Exportation. 1846–48.

An Appeal to Fallen Women. 1847.

Works. 1847–67.

The Haunted Man and the Ghost's Bargain: A Fancy for Christmas Time. 1848.

Elegy Written in a Country Churchyard. c. 1849.

The Personal History, Adventures, Experiences and Observations of David Copperfield the Younger. 1849–50.

Mr. Nightingale's Diary: A Farce (with Mark Lemon). 1851.

Bleak House. 1852–53.

A Child's History of England. 1852–54.

Hard Times, for These Times. 1854.

Little Dorrit. 1855–57.

Novels and Tales Reprinted from Household Words (editor). 1856–59.

The Case of the Reformers in the Literary Fund (with others). 1858.

Works (Library Edition). 1858–59, 1861–74

A Tale of Two Cities. 1859.

Christmas Stories from Household Words. 1859.

Great Expectations. 1861.

Great Expectations: A Drama. 1861.

The Uncommercial Traveller. 1861.

Our Mutual Friend. 1864–65.

The Frozen Deep (with Wilkie Collins). 1866.

No Thoroughfare (with Wilkie Collins). 1867.

Works (Charles Dickens Edition). 1867–75.

Christmas Stories from All the Year Round. c. 1868.

The Readings of Mr. Charles Dickens, as Condensed by Himself. 1868.

A Curious Dance round a Curious Tree (with W. H. Wills). 1870.

The Mystery of Edwin Drood. 1870.

Speeches Literary and Social. Ed. R. H. Shepherd. 1870.

The Newsvendors' Benevolent and Provident Institution: Speeches in Behalf of the Institution. 1871.

Is She His Wife? or Something Singular: A Comic Burletta. c. 1872.

The Lamplighter: A Farce. 1879.

The Mudfog Papers, etc. 1880.

Letters. Ed. Georgina Hogarth and Mary Dickens. 1880–1882.

Plays and Poems, with a Few Miscellanies in Prose Now First Collected. Ed. R. H. Shepherd. 1885.

The Lazy Tour of Two Idle Apprentices; No Thoroughfare; The Perils of Certain English Prisoners (with Wilkie Collins). 1890.

Works (Macmillan Edition). 1892–1925.

Letters to Wilkie Collins 1851–1870. Ed. Lawrence Hutton. 1892.

Works (Gadshill Edition). Ed. Andrew Lang. 1897–1908.

To Be Read at Dusk and Other Stories, Sketches and Essays. Ed. F. G. Kitton. 1898.

Christmas Stories from Household Words and All the Year Round. 1898.

Works (Biographical Edition). Ed. Arthur Waugh. 1902–03.

Poems and Verses. Ed. F. G. Kitton. 1903.

Works (National Edition). Ed. Bertram W. Matz. 1906–08.

Dickens and Maria Beadnell: Private Correspondence. Ed. G. P. Baker. 1908.

The Dickens-Kolle Letters. Ed. Harry B. Smith. 1910.

Works (Centenary Edition). 1910–11.

Dickens as Editor: Letters Written by Him to William Henry Wills, His Sub-Editor. Ed. R. C. Lehmann. 1912.

Works (Waverley Edition). 1913–18.

Unpublished Letters to Mark Lemon. Ed. Walter Dexter. 1927.

Letters to the Baroness Burdett-Coutts. Ed. Charles C. Osborne. 1931.

Dickens to His Oldest Friend: The Letters of a Lifetime to Thomas Beard. Ed. Walter Dexter. 1932.

Letters to Charles Lever. Ed. Flora V. Livingston. 1933.

Mr. and Mrs. Charles Dickens: His Letters to Her. Ed. Walter Dexter. 1935.

The Love Romance of Dickens, Told in His Letters to Maria Beadnell (Mrs. Winter). Ed. Walter Dexter. 1936.

The Nonesuch Dickens. Ed. Arthur Waugh, Hugh Walpole, Walter Dexter, and Thomas Hatton. 1937–38.

Letters. Ed. Walter Dexter. 1938.

Speeches. Ed. K. J. Fielding, 1960, 1988.

Letters (Pilgrim Edition). Ed. Madeline House, Graham Storey, Kathleen Tillotson et al. 1965– .

The Clarendon Dickens. Ed. John Butt, Kathleen Tillotson, and James Kinsley. 1966– .

Uncollected Writings from Household Words 1850–1859. Ed. Harry Stone. 1968.

Works about Charles Dickens

Ackroyd, Peter. *Dickens*. New York: Harper Collins, 1990.

Barnard, Robert. *Imagery and Theme in the Novels of Dickens*. Oslo: Universitetsforlaget, 1974.

Bloom, Harold, ed. *Charles Dickens*, Modern Critical Views. Philadelphia: Chelsea House Publishers, 1987.

———, ed. *A Tale of Two Cities*, Modern Critical Interpretations. Philadelphia: Chelsea House Publishers, 1987.

———, ed. *Charles Dickens*, Bloom's Major Novelists. Philadelphia: Chelsea House Publishers, 2000.

———, ed. *Great Expectations*, Modern Critical Interpretations. Philadelphia: Chelsea House Publishers, 2000.

Brook, George L. *The Language of Dickens*. London: Andre Deutsch, 1970.

Butt, John, and Kathleen Tillotson. *Dickens at Work*. London: Chatto & Windus, 1958.

Carey, John. *The Violent Effigy: A Study of Dickens' Imagination*. London: Faber & Faber, 1973.

Carlisle, Janice. *The Sense of an Audience: Dickens, Thackeray, and George Eliot at Mid-Century*. Athens: University of Georgia Press, 1981.

Chesterton, G.K. *Appreciations and Criticisms of the Works of Charles Dickens*. London: J.M. Dent & Sons, 1911.

———. *Charles Dickens*. London: House of Stratus, 2001. (Copyright by the Royal Literary Fund.)

Cockshut, A.O.J. *The Imagination of Charles Dickens.* New York: New York University Press, 1962.

Collins, Phillip, ed. *Dickens: The Critical Heritage.* London: Routledge & Kegan Paul, 1971.

Daldry, Graham. *Charles Dickens and the Form of the Novel.* Totowa, NJ: Barnes & Noble, 1987.

Dyson, A.E. *The Inimitable Dickens: A Reading of the Novels.* London: Macmillan, 1970.

Fielding, K.J. *Charles Dickens: A Critical Introduction.* London: Longmans, Green, 1958.

Ford, George H. *Dickens and His Readers.* Princeton University Press, 1955.

————, and Lauriat Lane Jr., eds. *The Dickens Critics.* Cornell University Press, 1961.

Forster, John. *The Life of Charles Dickens.* London: Whitefriars Press, 1928. Reprint.

Frank, Lawrence. *Charles Dickens and the Romantic Self.* Lincoln: University of Nebraska Press, 1984.

Gilbert, Elliot L. " 'To Awake from History': Carlyle, Thackeray, and *A Tale of Two Cities.*" *Dickens Studies Annual* 12 (1983): 247-65.

Gissing, George. *Charles Dickens.* New York: Dodd, Mead and Co., 1924.

————. *The Immortal Dickens.* London: Cecil Palmer, 1925.

Gold, Joseph. *Charles Dickens: Radical Moralist.* Minneapolis: University of Minnesota Press, 1972.

Goldberg, Michael. *Carlyle and Dickens.* Athens: University of Georgia Press, 1972.

Guerard, Albert J. *The Triumph of the Novel: Dickens, Dostoevsky, Faulkner.* New York: Oxford University Press, 1976.

Hardy, Barbara. *The Moral Art of Dickens.* New York: Oxford University Press, 1970.

Hawes, Donald, *Who's who in Dickens.* New York: Routledge, 2002

Herst, Beth R. *The Dickens Hero: Selfhood and Alienation in the Dickens World.* New York: AMS Press, 1990.

Holbrook, David. *Charles Dickens and the Image of Woman.* New York: New York University Press, 1993.

Hornback, Bert G. *"Noah's Arkitecture": A Study of Dickens's Mythology*. Athens: Ohio University Press, 1972.

Houston, Gail Turley. *Consuming Fictions; Gender, Class, and Hunger in Dickens's Novels*. Carbondale: Southern Illinois University Press, 1994.

House, Madeline, ed. *The Letters of Charles Dickens* (vols 1–8). Reprinted by Oxford University Press, 1965.

Ingham, Patricia. *Dickens, Women, and Language*. Toronto: University of Toronto Press, 1992.

John, Juliet, *Dickens's Villains: Melodrama, Character, Popular Culture*. Oxford: Oxford University Press, 2001

Johnson, Edgar H. *Charles Dickens: His Tragedy and Triumph*. Rev. ed. London: Allen Lane, 1977.

Jordan, John O., *the Cambridge Companion to Charles Dickens*. Cambridge: Cambridge University Press, 2001.

Kaplan, Fred. *Dickens: A Biography*. New York: William Morrow & Company, 1988.

Kincaid, James R. *Dickens and the Rhetoric of Laughter*. Oxford: Clarendon Press, 1971.

Kucich, John. *Excess and Restraint in the Novels of Charles Dickens*. Athens: University of Georgia Press, 1981.

Leavis, F.R., and Q.D. Leavis. *Dickens the Novelist*. London: Chatto & Windus, 1970.

Lettis, Richard. *The Dickens Aesthetic*. New York: AMS Press, 1989.

Lucas, John. *The Melancholy Man: A Study of Dickens's Novels*. Totowa, NJ: Barnes & Noble, 1980.

Manning, Sylvia Bank. *Dickens as Satirist*. New Haven: Yale University Press, 1971.

Miller, J. Hillis. *Charles Dickens: The World of His Novels*. Cambridge, MA: Harvard University Press, 1958.

Miyoshi, Masao. *The Divided Self: A Perspective on the Literature of the Victorians*. New York: New York University Press, 1969.

Monod, Sylvere. *Dickens the Novelist*. Norman: University of Oklahoma Press, 1968.

Morgan, Nicholas H. *Secret Journeys: Theory and Practice in Reading Dickens*. Rutherford, NJ: Fairleigh Dickinson University Press, 1992.

Nayder, Lillian, *Unequal Partners: Charles Dickens, Wilkie Collins, and Victorian Authorship*. Ithaca: Cornell University Press, 2002.

Neely, Robert D., *The Lawyers of Dickens and their Clerks*. Union: Lawbook Exchange, 2001.

Nelson, Harland S. *Charles Dickens*. Boston: Twayne, 1981.

Newcomb, Mildred. *The Imagined World of Charles Dickens*. Columbus: Ohio State University Press, 1989.

Nisber, Ada, and Blake Nevius, eds. *Dickens Centennial Essays*. Berkeley: University of California Press, 1971.

Page, Norman. *A Dickens Companion*. London: Macmillan, 1984.

Praz, Mario. "Charles Dickens." Praz's *The Hero in Eclipse in Victorian Fiction*. Tr. Angus Davidson. London: Oxford University Press, 1956, pp. 127-88.

Raina, Badri. *Dickens and the Dialectic of Growth*. Madison: University of Wisconsin Press, 1986.

Schad, John. *The Reader in the Dickensian Mirror: Some New Language*. New York: St. Martin's Press, 1992.

Schilling, Bernard N., *Rain of Years: Great Expectations and the World of Dickens*. Rochester: University of Rochester Press, 2001.

Schwarzbach, F.W. *Dickens and the City*. London: Athione Press, 1979.

Slater, Michael, ed. *Dickens 1970: Centenary Essays*. London: Chapman & Hall, 1970.

Solomon, Pearl Chesler. *Dickens and Melville in Their Time*. New York: Columbia University Press, 1975.

Spence, Gordon. "Dickens as a Historical Novelist." *Dickensian* 72 (1976): 21-30.

Stewart, Garrett. *Dickens and the Trials of Imagination*. Cambridge, MA: Harvard University Press, 1974.

Stoehr, Taylor. *Dickens: The Dreamer's Stance*. Ithaca, NY: Cornell University Press, 1965.

Stone, Harry. *Dickens and the Invisible World: Fairy Tales, Fantasy, and Novel-Making*. Bloomington: Indiana University Press, 1979.

———. *The Night Side of Dickens: Cannibalism, Passion, Necessity*. Columbus: Ohio State University Press, 1994.

Sucksmith, Harvey Peter. *The Narrative Art of Charles Dickens*. Oxford: Clarendon Press, 1970.

Thurley, Geoffrey. *The Dickens Myth: Its Genesis and Structure*. London: Routledge & Kegan Paul, 1976.

Tomalin, Claire. *The Invisible Woman: The Story of Nelly Ternan and Charles Dickens*. Viking, 1990.

Vogel, Jane. *Allegory in Dickens*. Mobile: University of Alabama Press, 1977.

Wall, Stephen, ed. *Charles Dickens: A Critical Anthology*. Penguin, 1970.

Welsh, Alexander. *The City of Dickens*. Oxford: Clarendon Press, 1971.

——. *From Copyright to Copperfield: The Identity of Dickens*. Cambridge, MA: Harvard University Press, 1987.

Williams, Raymond. *The English Novel: From Dickens to Lawrence*. London: Chatto & Windus, 1970.

Wilson, Angus. *The World of Charles Dickens*. New York: Viking, 1970.

Wilson, Edmund. "Two Scrooges." *The Wound and the Bow*. New York: Oxford University Press, 1947.

WEBSITES

Charles Dickens Gad's Hill Page
www.perryweb.com/Dickens/

Charles Dickens Heritage foundation
www.dickensfoundation.org/

Charles Dickens Museum
www.charlesdickensbirthplace.co.uk/

David Purdue's Charles Dickens Page
www.fidnet.com/~dap1955/dickens/

The Dickens Project
humwww.ucsc.edu/dickens/

Dickens Quarterly
www.umass.edu/english/dickens/

The Dickens Society
www.lang.nagoya-u.ac.jp/~matsuoka/Dickens-Society.html

Contributors

HAROLD BLOOM is Sterling Professor of the Humanities at Yale University and Henry W. and Albert A. Berg Professor of English at the New York University Graduate School. He is the author of over 20 books, including *Shelley's Mythmaking* (1959), *The Visionary Company* (1961), *Blake's Apocalypse* (1963), *Yeats* (1970), *A Map of Misreading* (1975), *Kabbalah and Criticism* (1975), *Agon: Toward a Theory of Revisionism* (1982), *The American Religion* (1992), *The Western Canon* (1994), and *Omens of Millennium: The Gnosis of Angels, Dreams, and Resurrection* (1996). *The Anxiety of Influence* (1973) sets forth Professor Bloom's provocative theory of the literary relationships between the great writers and their predecessors. His most recent books include *Shakespeare: The Invention of the Human*, a 1998 National Book Award finalist, and *How to Read and Why*, which was published in 2000. In 1999, Professor Bloom received the prestigious American Academy of Arts and Letters Gold Medal for Criticism.

MARIE TENNENT SHEPHARD has contributed to a number of children's educational magazines, and has written one other biography, *Maria Montessori: Teacher of Teachers*.

MEI CHIN is a writer living in New York City.

HENRY JAMES was a famed novelist, playright, essayist, short story writer, and critic. He was born to the American philosopher William

James. Besides being prolific, he was also one of the most famous 20th century American literary expatriates, and also one of the most famous early-modern writers. In James, wit and sophistication combine with a decadent and sometimes baffling prose, characters who are both subdued and sadistic, situations that are either commonplace or supernatural, and an obsessive love for sensuousness and detail. Perhaps today he is most widely read for his novels, of which he wrote twenty, including *Washington Square, Portrait of a Lady, What Maisie Knew, The Golden Bowl, The Ambassadors*, and *The Wings of a Dove*.

G. K. CHESTERTON, critic, poet, and novelist is now most well-known for his Father Brown mysteries, but whose short studies, especially of Chaucer, Dickens, and Robert Browning, are garnering renewed enthusiasm.

GEORGE GISSING was a novelist and critic, who was known for his portraits of the working-class, but is now more read for his commentary on Dickens, in *Charles Dickens* and *The Immortal Dickens*. Perhaps his most widely read novel today is *New Grub Street*. Like his hero Balzac, he wrote a massive novel series (22 books in all), beginning with *Workers in the Dawn*. Gissing had a struggling life, barely ever rising above poverty. His first wife was a prostitute, his second wife a servant.

INDEX

NOTE: In all cases, Dickens without a modifier refers to Charles Dickens. An "*n*" following a page number indicates an endnote.

Allan Woodcourt, 75
Esther Summerson
  complicated and understated, 66
  coy and manipulative, 68–69
  home is always Bleak House, 75
  narration of, 77
  Pip compared to, 116
  subtlest of Dickens' heroines, 67
Harold Skimpole, 77, 123
Inspector Bucket, 2, 118
Jo, 75
John Jarndyce, 2, 76, 119
Lady Dedlock, 76, 117
Lawrence Boythorn, 123
Lord Dedlock (Sir Leicester), 76,
  119–120
Mademoiselle Hortense, 2
Mr. Krook, 74
Mr. Turveytop, 77
Mr. Vholes, 118
Mrs. Jellyby, 77
Richard Carstone, 76, 121
"Bloomsburg Christening" (Dickens),
  23
Boz (pseudonym), 22, 25, 39–40. See
  also Sketches by Boz
British Museum Reading Room, 19
Browne, Hablot "Phiz," 28, 33–34, 35
Browning, Robert, 29
Burnett, Henry and Fanny Hogarth,
  34

Carlyle, Thomas, 25, 29
"The Cat's-Meat Man" (song), 11
Chapman and Hall
  Dickens' payments reduced by, 4
  exclusive publishers of Dickens, 36
  Nimrod Club cartoons, 26–27
  purchase rights to Sketches by Boz,
    31
Characters, list of. See also Dickens'
  characters, in general
Ada Clare, 32, 76

Agnes, 48, 62, 65–66, 71
Alice Marlow, 113–114
Allan Woodcourt, 75
Amy Dorrit, 50, 66, 77, 87
Artful Dodger (Jack Dawkins), 61
Arthur Clenham, 50, 72, 77, 87
Augustus Snodgrass, 27
Barnaby Rudge, 125
Bella Wilfer, 85
Betsy Trotwood, 65, 66
Bill Sikes, 106
Bob Cratchit, 4–5
Bob Fagin, 58, 75, 85
boys of Dotheboys Hall, 61
Bradley Headstone, 93–94, 117
Bumpls, 19
Captain Cuttle, 123
Charley Bates, 61
Charlie Hexam, 117
Cousin Feenix, 120
Cratchit family, 4–5
Crisparkle, 119
Daniel Quilp. See Daniel Quilp
  under The Old Curiosity Shop
David Copperfield. See David
  Copperfield under David
  Copperfield, characters in
Dick Swiveller, 36, 62, 85
Dolly Vardon, 37
Dora, 48, 64–65, 70, 87, 99
Edith Dombey, 69, 76, 117
Estella, 52, 82
Esther Summerson. See Esther
  Summerson under Bleak House,
  characters in
Eugene Wrayburn, 84, 85, 93–94
Flora Flinching, 50, 59, 72
Florence Dombey, 62
Harold Skimpole, 77, 123
Helena Landless, 59
Herbert Pocket, 71, 78, 120–121
Inspector Bucket, 2, 118
Jo, 75
Joe Gargery, 80–81, 109–110, 122